We all want it all. Which one of us has ever said we want only some of it? Not I. But saying it and achieving it are two very different things. As a senior business executive, single mom, bestie, daughter, sister, professor, entrepreneur, and author, I have more titles than I can count, and I want more accomplishments than my twenty-four-hour day tells me I can have, so that is why *this* book is key. I want to do it all well. Touré Roberts lays out vulnerable, honest, practical, and applicable advice on how to do it. You can take it or leave it. I'm taking it. And I highly recommend that you take it too. Immediately.

—**Bozoma St. John,** chief marketing officer, Netflix

With *Balance*, Touré Roberts takes us on an epic journey of self-discovery and brilliantly redefines our understanding of Balance. This is the ultimate guide on how to tap into the highest, most powerful version of yourself. It's a must-read for anyone ready to break free from the chaos of their life and into the clarity of their destiny.

—**DeVon Franklin,** Hollywood producer;
*New York Times* bestselling author

At one of the lowest points of my life, Pastor Touré, with his words and guidance, lifted me out of a dark place. I thought I'd been buried, and it was hard to see beyond the darkness, but what I realized through his words is that I'd been planted (not buried). It was my time to sow, and the time for reaping would come; surely enough, it did. Touré helped me find Balance and think positively; he encouraged me to question the narrative that I was feeding myself that was not serving me. Our biggest setback is often not what others say about us but the story we tell ourselves.

—**Anjula Acharia,** CEO, A-Series Management and Investments

Touré Roberts is one of our most valued thought-provokers, and his book *Balance* couldn't have come at a better time. No matter where you are on your journey, you'll grow from this book, becoming a greater you.

—**Common,** Golden Globe, Oscar, and Grammy award–
winning rapper and actor; *New York Times* bestselling author

Most of us feel overwhelmed with too much to do and no idea what to do about it. Thankfully my friend Touré Roberts has written a very helpful, soul-settling, priority-clarifying, life-altering book called *Balance*. But before you read it, let me caution you. A truly balanced life may not be what you think it is. If you find yourself ready for a change, this book will help bring out your best.

—**Craig Groeschel,** pastor, Life.Church; *New York Times* bestselling author

Right on time! Thankful for this new meditation on Balance from one of the preeminent spiritual teachers of our day. A focusing and engaging work with some of the most practical application you'll find anywhere. Thanking God for the revelation and equilibrium found in *Balance*.

—**Leslie Odom Jr.,** Tony and Grammy award–winning actor and singer

# BALANCE

# Also by Touré Roberts

*Purpose Awakening: Discover the Epic Idea That Motivated Your Birth*

*Wholeness: Winning in Life from the Inside Out*

# BALANCE

POSITIONING YOURSELF

TO DO ALL THINGS WELL

## TOURÉ ROBERTS

ZONDERVAN
BOOKS

ZONDERVAN BOOKS

*Balance*
Copyright © 2022 by Touré Roberts

Requests for information should be addressed to:
Zondervan, *3900 Sparks Dr. SE, Grand Rapids, Michigan 49546*

Zondervan titles may be purchased in bulk for educational, business, fundraising, or sales promotional use. For information, please email SpecialMarkets@Zondervan.com.

ISBN 978-0-310-35984-5 (international trade paper edition)
ISBN 978-0-310-35983-8 (audio)

---

Library of Congress Cataloging-in-Publication Data

Names: Roberts, Touré, author.
Title: Balance : positioning yourself to do all things well / Touré Roberts.
Description: Grand Rapids : Zondervan, 2022. | Includes bibliographical references. | Summary: "Popular speaker and national bestselling author Touré Roberts presents a complete guide that informs, inspires, and teaches the critical discipline of learning to make the necessary spiritual, mental, relational, and even professional adjustments required to be the best version of yourselves in a world of constant change"— Provided by publisher.
Identifiers: LCCN 2022000591 (print) | LCCN 2022000592 (ebook) | ISBN 9780310359814 (hardcover) | ISBN 9780310359821 (ebook)
Subjects: LCSH: Work-life balance. | Quality of life. | Awareness—Religious aspects.
Classification: LCC HD4094.25 .R63 2022 (print) | LCC HD4094.25 (ebook) | DDC 658—dc23/eng/20220131
LC record available at https://lccn.loc.gov/2022000591
LC ebook record available at https://lccn.loc.gov/2022000592

---

Scripture quotations are taken from the New King James Version®. Copyright © 1982 by Thomas Nelson. Used by permission. All rights reserved.

Any internet addresses (websites, blogs, etc.) and telephone numbers in this book are offered as a resource. They are not intended in any way to be or imply an endorsement by Zondervan, nor does Zondervan vouch for the content of these sites and numbers for the life of this book.

The author is represented by Dupree Miller and Associates.

*Cover photography: Micah Kandros*
*Cover design: Amanda McIntire*
*Author photo: Micah Kandros*
*Interior design: Denise Froehlich*

*Printed in the United States of America*

---

22 23 24 25 26 / LSC / 10 9 8 7 6 5 4 3 2 1

*To my children, Ren, Teya, Isaiah,*
*Malachi, Makenzie, and Ella*

As with every book I write, I thought of
you and the tools that will help you live the
most healthy, productive, rewarding, and
impactful life possible. My prayer is that
this book adds value each time you read it.
You are my forever inspiration. I love you!

# Contents

*Foreword by Sarah Jakes Roberts*. . . . . . . . . . . . . . . . . . . . . . xi

Introduction: Balance Isn't What You Think It Is . . . . . . . . . . . 1

## Part 1: Redefining Balance

1. The Midnight Sun . . . . . . . . . . . . . . . . . . . . . . . . . . . . . 7
2. There's No Team in "I". . . . . . . . . . . . . . . . . . . . . . . . . .21
3. What the Soul Craves . . . . . . . . . . . . . . . . . . . . . . . . . 37
4. The Gift of Rest. . . . . . . . . . . . . . . . . . . . . . . . . . . . . 55

## Part 2: Restoring Balance

5. Five Signs of Imbalance . . . . . . . . . . . . . . . . . . . . . . . 71
6. The Power of No . . . . . . . . . . . . . . . . . . . . . . . . . . . . 85
7. Balance after the Blow . . . . . . . . . . . . . . . . . . . . . . . . 99

## Part 3: Refining Balance

8. Surrendering to Peace . . . . . . . . . . . . . . . . . . . . . . . .117
9. The Balanced Day . . . . . . . . . . . . . . . . . . . . . . . . . . 133
10. Protecting Balance. . . . . . . . . . . . . . . . . . . . . . . . . . .149

Afterword. . . . . . . . . . . . . . . . . . . . . . . . . . . . . . . . . . . .167

*Acknowledgments* . . . . . . . . . . . . . . . . . . . . . . . . . . . . .173

*Notes*. . . . . . . . . . . . . . . . . . . . . . . . . . . . . . . . . . . . . .175

# Foreword by Sarah Jakes Roberts

Long before his fingertips became obedient to the idea that had formed in his mind, I watched Touré Roberts labor over this book. Of course, I didn't realize it in the moment, but now I see it so clearly. The pivots and adjustments he made for himself and for our marriage, family, ministries, and businesses were a surrender to a deeper knowing that no one could fully see but him. The substance of those moments has transformed into the wisdom you hold in your hands.

I can remember the first time I witnessed him break the rhythm of our life so that we could address what the soul of our family needed. We were early into our blended family life. The children weren't fussing, but you could sense the awkward tension of strangers trying to become family. I was a few months pregnant, and my hormones were forcing anyone within reach to strap in for an emotional roller-coaster ride.

Years ago, on Saturday night the house was teeming with tension. The walls were undoubtedly placing bets on who would explode in exasperation first. I was looking for clothing that would accommodate my changing body, while calculating what time I'd need to leave with the children to make it on time for church the next morning. Touré ventured into the closet, took one look at me, and said, "I don't think we should go to church tomorrow."

I was appalled. Church was the one thing I was counting on

to diffuse the thick layer of tension in our home. Not to mention, everyone coming to service was expecting to hear from the very man who suggested we not attend at all. Before I could explain to him all the reasons we should go, he'd already made the phone call excusing himself from the platform. "Instead we'll have a family day," he said.

Before the family day activities could commence, the house felt lighter and freer. Literally overnight our home became sacred, and our group of little strangers took one step closer to becoming a family. This didn't happen because we missed a church service. It occurred because Touré took our lives off autopilot and dared to be still enough to hear what the soul of our family was crying out for.

I could share with you countless sensitive-leadership moments like this. Moments when Touré dared to stop doing what we've always done and chose to lean into the possibilities that could exist within our present moment.

I have watched him live out every lesson, nugget, revelation, and breakthrough laid out in this book. For more than a year he has taken the time to extrapolate with keen precision, brilliance, and commitment the pivotal, identity-shifting moments that exposed our family, ministries, and organizations to a limitless existence.

I have always known that what I received daily needed to reach the hands of as many people as possible. Too many are showing up in their lives but haven't taken the time to reassess what is feasible for who they are now.

No wonder we find ourselves feeling so out of balance. How you do what you do and why you do what you do is ever evolving. It's not always what you do that needs changing; sometimes it's how you accomplish it that can be modified. Then there are moments when it's less about how you achieve a goal and more about why the goal matters in the first place.

You could not have a better guide than my husband and friend to help you discover the individualized expression of balance that your world needs. I am the chief beneficiary of the wisdom that resides in these pages. I am confident that this is a lifelong companion manual for living an unapologetically free, firm, awakened, and powerful life, from a man who has embodied the message.

More than a book, this is a key to unlocking the greatest gift you can give yourself and the world that you serve: the most balanced version of you. Farewell to autopilot and feeling like your world could just keep spinning until it's out of control. Your days of running on fumes with no fuel in sight are over. You will never be without again.

# Introduction

## *Balance Isn't What You Think It Is*

*Next to love, balance is the most important thing.*
—JOHN WOODEN

This is not your best."

Not exactly what you want to hear from your literary agent after submitting a sample chapter of your new book. But she was right; it wasn't my best, and deep down I knew it. Like the hamster on the wheel, I had been working so hard but wondered if I was getting anywhere. As if delivering a manuscript on a tight timeline weren't enough, I was steering several organizations, which I lead, through a global pandemic, having to pivot all of our in-person operations to online-only to stay afloat. The world had changed in one day, and in hindsight, how silly it was of me to think that everything around me could change without requiring a deep inner reset in order for me to perform optimally.

Everything had changed yet I just kept going, according to the notion of perseverance. But my output was slipping badly, and my agent, thank God, called me on it. "Touré. This is not your best. I'm calling your publisher and getting you more time, and you are going

1

to take time off and clear your head so that you can bring all of yourself to this book!"

Her remedy should not have surprised me, but still, how could I not feel like the biggest hypocrite in the world? Here I was, writing a book about balance, promising to show others the way during a time when I probably had never been more out of balance in my own life. How insane, right? Thankfully, though, the truth always has a way of challenging us if we are humble enough to listen, and what was made painfully clear to me was that I had much more to learn about balance than I realized.

Although my agent's words were jarring, at the same time they were deeply liberating. I knew that something was off with me, but I could not pinpoint it, let alone access a remedy. In the midst of juggling and accommodating and recalibrating and improvising due to the pandemic and its collateral damage, I had lost my mojo, what I think of as my creative rhythm. Anytime I'm launching a new initiative, writing another book, developing a speech, preparing to lead a seminar or a staff or board meeting, I typically do so from a place of dynamic creative abundance. It may take a deep focus to get me there, but once I'm locked in, I usually discover far more creative resources and capacity than the task even requires. It's an overflow, a wellspring of sorts, that I'm able to access, and when I tap into it, miracles—sometimes literally—happen. What I've learned to call balance now, though, no longer looks like what I once assumed balance must be.

I had been pursuing time management strategies, struggling in the art of juggling, but what I should have been pursuing was authentic balance. I was soon awakened to the reality that my new projects, and the exemplary fulfillment of everything else I was trying to accomplish, would emerge only from a new place of balance in my life. My creativity, my relational success, my innovation, my effectiveness, my profitability—everything that I was after was waiting for me in this new pivot point.

So, my friend, I suspect that balance is likely not what you too have come to assume it is. To recover my equilibrium during an upside-down, roller-coaster season of life, I had to redefine balance in my life and discover something more than new time management apps and constant guilt over my lack of work-life balance. Consequently, however, I believe I have much more to share with you about restoring balance to your life than you might be expecting. The journey to balance navigated by this book goes far deeper than the popular theme of work-life balance that we've been exposed to, although those principles are sometimes helpful. The balance that we will cover together affirms getting your work and life in sync but goes beyond being home in time for dinner, regular scheduled date nights, and quality time with the kids.

Balance is not about learning to effectively give pieces of yourself to important things. It's about knowing and becoming all of yourself and then giving your whole, abundant self to everything and everyone your life is assigned to.

Balance will teach you how to align with the highest version of yourself in any given moment. A version of you that, among many other things, replaces anxiety with peace, dysfunction with progress, and stagnation with unlimited creativity.

That's what this book is all about. You will discover throughout these pages that life uses every moment in our existence—especially the chaotic ones—to nudge us toward a greater version of ourselves, which in turn produces extraordinary experiences. My belief is that the message in these pages will unlock that ability within you to discover a new method of balancing all the areas of your life.

We will explore in detail that idea that Balance is actually a spiritual location and requires spiritual means and spiritual insights to get there. We'll get into that later. Perhaps the first step on this journey is no step at all but simply a pause to stop and perceive where you are. This sounds easier than it is, because hitting pause means taking a deep breath and turning down the volume on all the clamor in your busy life.

The more in touch with balance I've become, the more I've realized how noisy life is, with no sign of quieting anytime soon. Perhaps one of the reasons why self-awareness and mindfulness have become cultural buzzwords is in part because people are trying to manage the noise. The world's population is constantly growing while technology is making the world smaller and smaller. This expansive shrinking makes our lives more and more crowded. We are increasingly exposed to the lives, thoughts, opinions, issues, and passions of countless strangers simply by going online and scrolling our social media accounts. I promise not to add to the overcrowded playlist of your life but to help you listen to the whispers of your heart.

The journey *to* balance is the beginning *of* balance. The moment you picked up this book, you were responding to your soul's yearning for wholeness, rest, and fulfillment. I'm thrilled to lead you through these pages on your voyage to balance, and my prayer is that you will enthusiastically move onward and upward to being the best, blessed, and most balanced version of yourself.

Welcome home, my friend!

Welcome to discovering or perhaps, if you're like me, rediscovering your absolute best!

# PART 1

# REDEFINING
# BALANCE
BALANCE
BALANCE
BALANCE

# CHAPTER 1

# The Midnight Sun

*Here is an unspeakable secret: Paradise is all around us and we do not understand.*

—THOMAS MERTON

The sun blazes from the center of the pale-blue, cloudless sky above, its glare reflected off the waters just beyond the beach. Time stands still as you stroll along the shoreline, allowing the warmth overhead to soak into your skin. After walking for a mile or so, you pause and notice how the horizon seems to glow in a radiant band that's almost white above the edge of the sea. The sun appears to remain fixed in place, right where it was an hour ago. You yawn and smile and check your watch. It's 3:00 a.m., even though it feels more like 3:00 p.m.

No, this isn't a dream or fantasy—this is reality in the lands of the midnight sun.

The natural phenomenon of the midnight sun happens twice annually as the earth rotates at a tilted angle while circling the sun. At one part of the earth's orbit, the sun shines continuously north of the arctic circle, and at the opposite part, it shines continuously south of the antarctic circle. During their summers, some parts of the world enjoy endless sunshine for several months. These places include Reykjavík, Iceland; Svalbard, Norway; Abisko, Sweden; Whitehorse, Canada; and Fairbanks, Alaska. While the sun does appear to move across the sky, it never sets the way most of us are accustomed to seeing. Instead it dips to kiss the horizon and begins to rise again.

Just imagine the sun remaining visible both day and night.

## The Happiest Place on Earth

Imagine going through your daily routine, waking up, dressing, exercising, eating breakfast, going to work, running errands, helping the kids with homework, meeting a friend for dinner, coming home, putting the kids to bed, reading a book, getting in bed, watching television, yawning, going to sleep, waking up the next morning and starting again. You've completed an entire twenty-four-hour cycle; however, something was different. There was no darkness. The light around you remained constant—a significant contrast to what most people in the world experience!

Think about all the things you might accomplish if you weren't hindered by darkness and nightfall. It would be like the break of dawn, only all the time. Can you see yourself living in ceaseless light? How would your life be different? How would you change your schedule?

The possibility thrills me because I love the dawn. Each new day it brings a message of hope, new beginnings, opportunities for redemption, new possibilities, and fresh inspiration for progress. In contrast, night comes and shrouds us in darkness. Even in the developed areas of the world, where electricity ensures artificial light anytime, people still experience stress, worry, and fear. Granted, the darkness of night can signal the need for our body to rest. But it can also present the perfect setting for our angst, anxiety, and panic attacks.

In those certain places, however, at least for a period of time ranging from a few weeks to a few months, the sun always shines. Curiously enough, many of those places—Norway, Sweden, Denmark, Finland, and Iceland—often rank in the top ten of the happiest places on earth. Various studies and annual assessments measure such things as quality of life, community satisfaction, relational contentment, security, and personal fulfillment. While these places also experience corresponding periods in winter in which they are in darkness even through the daytime, they consistently rank as places where the inhabitants feel happy and enjoy their quality of life. Considering that their cold, dark winters are balanced by a season with what must feel like eternal sunshine, it's no wonder they are so happy. It turns out, the happiest place on earth is not Disneyland; it's the place where the sun always shines!

## Goodbye, Night

I share my fascination with the midnight sun in order to illustrate the concept of balance. While I explored various other analogies to help describe my understanding of balance, none of them captivated my attention as did the vivid particulars of what it would be like to enjoy sunshine 24-7. Although I've experienced balance in the way that I want to share with you, it can be challenging to explain. Once you get it, your own internal light begins to shine, but getting it requires insight, revelation, and practice.

As we begin our journey to balance, we must first realize that balance is not a discipline, an activity, or an exercise. Balance is a place. That's right, Balance has a location, and going forward, when I refer to Balance—the place—I will capitalize it in order to distinguish it from the other notions and usages of balance. Those who find the location of Balance learn to live in it and experience its midnight sun, a never-diminishing light rich in the warmth of affirmation, the solid foundation of truth, clarity that dispels confusion, creativity that activates the impossible, more wisdom than they could ever apply, and of course, among many other things, let us not forget happiness.

Please allow me to be very clear. My reference to Balance as a place is not hyperbole. Balance really is a place, but perhaps in a way that is different from what you might first consider. You won't find Balance on a map, on a globe, or in an atlas. Balance isn't a physical place. It's a spiritual place within a spiritual dimension, and I can't imagine where or who I would be if I hadn't discovered the way into its wonders.

Balance is a place where the sun is always shining. There is no night there. In this environment of ever-present light, truth is continuously illuminated. Balance allows you to see yourself and those around you without the distortion and perversion that Night, the antagonist of Balance, introduces.

It's like waking up in a familiar room in the middle of the night and being frightened by the sinister shapes around you. A favorite hat appears to be the face of an unwelcome stranger. Once the light is turned on again in your room, you realize that you're safe and secure. It was only the darkness playing tricks on your mind. Sure, you'll be able to get back to sleep eventually, but only after reassuring yourself with what you know to be true. You not only lose some blissful sleep, but—most important—you lose the gift of peace that our lives were meant to be governed by.

Finding and remaining in Balance is important because darkness is expensive. Night wants us disoriented and distracted. If we aren't careful, Night will constantly steal from us and slowly chip away at our confidence. Night will make us fearful and cause us to procrastinate until we run out of time and forfeit our opportunities. If Night has its way, it will bankrupt our potential and leave us on the side of the road, disillusioned and discouraged, forgetting who we were born to become, gladly accepting any crumb that falls in our direction. To hell with Night!

## When Morning Comes

Night is a constant adversary of truth, whispering—and at times yelling—its favorite tune: "You're Not Enough." Night is obsessed with you, but not in a good way. It stalks you, calling you every name imaginable except your real name—your divine one. Night is a relentless foe and sometimes can feel undefeatable. But with only the slightest introduction of Day, illuminated by the first rays of light, Night flees like the thief it is.

Night is afraid of you because you are its master. That's right, you are light waiting to be unleashed. There are many levels to your brightness, and as you stand in the daylight of Balance, you constantly evolve until light permeates your entire being, pushing back every trace of Night in your life.

I remember a Bible passage that my childhood pastor would always quote: "Weeping may endure for a night, but joy comes in the morning."[1] Every time he would read that passage to the congregation, the room would erupt with enthusiasm. The truth implied offered the promise of hope: although their night season was causing them to weep, a breakthrough that would bring them joy was coming with daybreak. This was surely an encouraging thought, one that undoubtedly strengthened my faith when I was navigating difficult times, and for this I am very grateful. As I've grown in my understanding of Balance and the power therein, however, I've discovered a deeper insight into that passage, an insight that has helped me tremendously.

I believe we miss something when we equate morning—and Balance—only to a change in circumstances. This way of interpreting that passage suggests that the joy of morning can appear only the moment the doctor's report comes back negative or that dawn can show up only when the financial miracle arrives. This would mean that there will be no daylight unless there is a dramatic turn in the right direction in your marriage or relationship. Essentially, this would mean that our morning is subject to the discretion of our night. But my experience with Balance has caused me to believe in a better reality.

I learned that I can play a part in determining when my morning comes and that the healing rays of the sun are always within reach. I discovered that I don't have to sit around weeping at the mercy of my nighttime circumstances. I found that I can induce my morning and find its joy in spite of my situation if I can simply get to the place where the morning never ends and the sun shines bright, even at midnight—the place called Balance.

## The Coordinates of Balance

You won't find the latitude and longitude for Balance on a map or with GPS on your phone. The place of Balance is indeed a spiritual location, and to get there requires spiritual means and insights. Once you begin this journey, you will discover that Balance is closer than you think.

Now, this is the part where things begin to get deep. You may be thinking, "Touré, I thought we were in deep already." Yeah . . . no. We're just getting started. There is no way around the process of digging deep within, perhaps deeper than you've ever considered, in order to experience and possess the irreplaceable life treasures that can be discovered only by living in Balance.

Now, I'll need you to allow me to stretch your senses and imagination some. Although this is not a religious book, it does necessitate an openness to deeper spiritual themes. Don't worry, you won't finish this book and find yourself barefoot, dressed in white linen, living in a commune on a secluded mountain, eating only raw fruits and vegetables and the fresh fish you reeled in that day from a nearby stream. This is not that type of party. This book, however, will challenge you to have a little faith and to consider more deeply the idea of purpose, destiny, and a divine plan at work concerning your life.

The rewards that finding Balance promises to bring into your life far outweigh the risks associated with putting on the table for your consideration themes and ideas that may or *may not* challenge where you presently are. Nothing here will be forced on you; I am against that. Everything will just be presented for you to ponder and process and see if it resonates. Once I discovered the wholeness of Balance, I was very intentional about writing this book in a way that ensures that its context and content proves profitable and applicable to everyone, no matter where these pages find them. Sound like a plan? So if you don't mind a little adventure, let's be on our way to growth, enrichment, and—most of all—Balance!

## Dig Deeper

The reason why we have to dig deep in order to begin our journey to Balance is because the path to Balance commences from within the deepest part of ourselves. The average person may not consider this, but every human is a multilayered being. There are so many dimensions to who we are. We have an outer dimension, which of course is our bodies—our physical selves—and we have an inner dimension, which includes our mind, our spirit, and our soul. I find it fascinating that although the outer and the inner are separate, they are uniquely interconnected and by design are dependent on each other for the purpose of each life becoming and accomplishing what it was created to be and do.

The brain is a part of the physical body and the tangible, outer dimension, yet it is inextricably connected to the mind part of your inner dimension. The brain is made up of blood vessels and nerve cells and has a definable shape and structure. The mind, on the other hand, is mental, intangible, and has no physical shape or structure, yet it creates movement in the brain. Of course, there have been debates on the difference between brain and mind since the time of Aristotle, but for me it comes down to this: the brain I can touch; the mind I cannot.

Your spirit is your inner person, the inner face of who you are. Yet the spirit of a person is just as distinguishable as the outer face of a person. The spirit is who that person is from the inside out, and just as with the correlation between mind and brain, a person's spirit will undoubtedly impact their physical life. The spirit of a person is who a person is. Their body can and will change, but their spirit will always be who they truly are.

You with me? Let me provide a very personal example. I have the most beautiful wife in the world. Without question she is physically gorgeous, so much so that I have to keep myself from howling when she walks past me in the kitchen—or anywhere, for that matter. My baby is a hot fox, no doubt, but her outer isn't what captivated me about her from the beginning; it was her spirit. Seriously, I noticed this from the start. During our first meeting to discuss some work that we could potentially do together, her inner being outshined her physical beauty. Her spirit was breathtaking. After just a few conversations and observations, I knew that she was the one. We connected spirit to spirit, and the rest was history. To be thorough, the spirit thing works also in the opposite direction. In times past I've met people with all of the right physical features to be gorgeous, but after drawing near to them and engaging with their spirit, I decided it best to *mosey on along*, if you know what I mean.

The spirit is where we initially connect with spiritual things. In my tradition, worship is a vital discipline, one I deeply enjoy, and I never leave a worship experience without floating on a cloud. For me, it's not about the kneeling, standing, gesturing, and many other physical expressions that some associate with worship. There's nothing wrong with doing any of those things, if that's your preference, and there are times in my worship moments when some of those are appropriate; however, if my spirit isn't engaged and connected to the experience, then I haven't worshiped at all. The spirit is the facilitator of spiritual things.

And then there's the soul.

The soul is the deepest part of our makeup. It is so deeply recessed within our inner dimension that the awareness of *its* existence often eludes us. Many have embraced the concept of being self-aware, yet too few are intentional about being *soul*-aware. Jesus himself tried to get his followers to understand this critical insight by asking, "What will it profit a man if he gains the whole world, and loses his own soul?"[2]

In essence he was saying that there is nothing more important or valuable in life than to discover your soul and to know it intimately. We are not profited, nor often *profitable*, when we've yet to discover or have lost our sense of soul. We cannot separate ourselves from our soul nor from the soul's activities. When we aren't soul-aware, we misinterpret what the soul is trying to accomplish, and we falsely translate its pursuit of fulfillment to the pursuit of physical things. If this tendency is left unchecked, we unfortunately end up gaining everything the physical world has to offer at the expense of being disconnected from and lost concerning the deepest and most powerful part of our makeup—our soul. I echo Jesus. This is not profitable. When it comes to the soul, ignorance is not bliss. Soul-awareness is a critical first step to finding Balance. Therefore, before we go farther, I'd like to take a moment and briefly discuss the difference between being self-aware and being soul-aware.

## Self-Awareness versus Soul-Awareness

Self-awareness has become an increasingly popular buzzword for anyone seeking to improve their lives, from CEOs and thought leaders to homemakers, tech programmers, and retail managers—and for good reason. According to a 2018 *Harvard Business Review* article by organizational psychologist, researcher, and bestselling author Tasha Eurich, PhD, internal self-awareness is described as how clearly we see ourselves. More specifically, how we see our values, passions, aspirations, thoughts, feelings, behaviors, strengths, and weaknesses, along with our impact on others.[3]

Eurich goes on to explain how research suggests that when we see ourselves clearly, we are more confident and creative. We make sounder decisions, build stronger relationships, and communicate more effectively. Self-aware people also tend to be better workers who get more promotions, and they are more likely to be better leaders. Clearly, being self-aware is a wonderful thing and a great step in the right direction;

however, what I'm talking about is much deeper and, because the fruit of being soul-aware is discovering Balance, much richer.

Being soul-aware encompasses all the benefits that being self-aware achieves and more, because learning to be in touch with and listening to your soul's need for Balance introduces you to a version of yourself far greater than the present you. Soul-awareness produces a you who is exceptional. Being soul-aware leads you to an environment where the light never ceases and the night and all its hindering boogeymen are chased away. Chains you didn't even know you carried dissolve, freeing you to go from just okay to good, from good to great, and from great to extraordinary. Soul-awareness fosters an environment that both reveals and gives expression to not just your best qualities but your divine nature.

Here's an interesting fact. According to that same *Harvard Business Review* article, the research showed that even though most believe they are self-aware, only 10–15 percent actually fit the criteria.[4] I wonder if the reason for this dramatic shortfall comes down to this: we will never be completely self-aware without reaching into the soul, the deepest part of self. Self-awareness without soul-awareness leaves blind spots and unnecessary limitations, but if you are soul-aware, self-awareness is a given.

Your soul is the most honest part of you. It is the ultimate truth of you. It is the most authentic version of you, yet not to be confused with the highest version of you. The authentic version of you is where you're at. The highest version of you is where you're going. The soul is clear about what it needs, where Balance is, and what it takes to get there. In the ideal scenario, the enlightened, soul-aware person learns to rule their spirit and mind, bringing both into submission to the mission of the soul.

## Music of the Soul

Your soul is after something. It isn't lying dormant. Like a magnet, the soul is drawn to Balance as the needle of a compass is to north. Its activity is a longing for the place of abundant peace, creativity, wisdom, innovation, virtue, strength, and ability. Our activity, in turn, must be to tap into and bring all of ourselves to this longing. Although this yearning of the soul happens within the deepest part of ourselves, with discipline we can surely access it. It starts with learning to dive deep beneath the layers of all of life's noise.

The more I grow in Balance, the more I recognize how noisy life is and is increasingly becoming. As I mentioned earlier, one of the reasons why self-awareness and mindfulness are such coveted goals is because, among other things, people are trying to manage the noise. It seemingly gets louder than we can manage, because the world's population is constantly growing while technology is making the world smaller and smaller. Consequently, our lives become more and more crowded. We are increasingly exposed to the life, thoughts, opinions, issues, comments, passions, and preferences of strangers simply by logging on to the internet and our social media accounts, with new platforms vying for our attention every day.

As a result, the noise of strangers adds to and amplifies our own noise, and with each day and each log-on the noise is compounded exponentially. There was a time when a person's noise was limited to what they had going on personally, along with the activities of family and close friends. That has changed drastically. And in many situations, we are no longer called people but are called users, and those who call us users are like pushers, spending billions of dollars on new ways to distract us and draw our attention to the products and services they want us to consume. More noise, louder and louder.

And then you've got the good noise: relationships, parenting, business, career, education, community service, and every other virtuous responsibility that makes for a happy and fulfilling life. That's all good, but guess what? It's still noise. And let us not forget the dark noise that Night speaks to us all. Those voices, within and without, that echo around us in the absence of light. Those bumps in the night and startling sounds we must overcome.

Life is indeed noisy, and often we don't even realize how noisy until we take the time to be still. To find Balance, you must learn the discipline of regularly muting life's noise. Tapping into the rhythm of the soul will require a diligent, consistent commitment to stillness. The rhythm of the soul is a faint pulse, but with the right kind of stillness it can be discovered, and when it is, the choreography that orders our steps to Balance reveals itself. As we walk through these pages together, we're going to find the most effective ways to do just that—to listen to the music of your soul and implement its tempo in the rhythms of your life.

# You Are Here

Before we move on to the next chapter, now is a good time to recap where we've been. Here are our key takeaways so far.

1. *Balance is a place within you*—not a discipline, self-improvement plan, activity, or exercise. It's not a physical place but a spiritual one, the atmosphere of which causes everything dark to fade, allowing the highest version of ourselves to emerge.
2. *Every person is a multilayered being.* There are many dimensions to who we are. We have our outer dimension, which includes our bodies—our physical selves—and we have our inner dimension, which includes our minds, our spirits, and our souls.
3. *The soul is the deepest part of our makeup.* It is so deeply recessed within the inner dimension of who we are that the awareness of its existence often requires internal exploration.
4. *Your soul is the most honest part of you.* It is the ultimate truth of you. It is the most authentic version of you, yet not to be confused with the highest version of you. The authentic version of you is where you are. The highest version of you is where you are going.

5. *Experiencing Balance requires soul-awareness,* the deepest and most comprehensive level of self-awareness.

6. *Self-awareness without soul-awareness has blind spots and limitations,* but if you are soul-aware, then the benefits of self-awareness are a given.

7. *The soul is drawn to Balance* as the needle of a compass is to true north. It longs for the place of abundant peace, creativity, wisdom, innovation, virtue, strength, and ability.

8. *The enlightened, soul-aware person learns to rule their spirit and mind,* bringing them into submission to the mission of the soul.

9. *Life is noisy and continually becoming noisier.* This noise disconnects us from ourselves. It distracts us and disrupts our pursuit of what will allow us to reside in Balance.

10. *Balance requires listening to your soul, not to the noise around you.* The person who will find Balance must learn the discipline of regularly muting life's noise. Learning effective ways of stillness allows us to tap into the rhythm of the soul, which leads us right into Balance.

Family, we're on our way to Balance! The moment you picked up this book, you were responding to your soul's yearning for the place where the sun never sets. I can already feel the midnight sun beginning to shine through in your life. It's time to step into the next phase of our journey, with Balance as our destination.

It only gets better from here!

# CHAPTER 2

# There's No Team in "I"

*Life is like riding a bicycle. To keep your balance, you must keep moving.*

—ALBERT EINSTEIN

One time my wife, Sarah, and I were driving through Dallas when we saw something that captivated us both. We were enjoying amazing weather that day, just the right amount of sun without that intense, sweltering heat that Texas knows how to serve up from time to time. A few clouds, a light breeze—it was just right.

Sarah and I pulled up to a stoplight, and there beside us were two stunning, tricked-out Harley-Davidson motorcycles being ridden by what will forever be, as far as I am concerned, the coolest couple in the entire world. Decked out in leather gear, this pair revved their engines in a manner that boldly suggested that the road—and I mean all of it—was theirs.

Total perfection. They took off, turned in unison, and her hair blew in the wind as their bikes cut through the breeze and blazed into the sunset. They were the JayZ and Beyoncé of bikers. What a sight to see! Sarah and I were so impressed, we turned to each other and voiced our thoughts. "We could totally do that!" At that moment, we decided that one day we were going to ride motorcycles together, determined to become that level of *couple-coolness*. Surely, that had to be one of the most amazing experiences that two people could have together.

# Riding Solo

For several weeks, whenever we'd see anyone riding a motorcycle, we would remind each other of the couple we saw and how we needed to take the steps toward learning to ride and, of course, how we needed to shop for a couple of motorcycles to realize our newfound dream. But as weeks turned into months, we talked about the possibility less and less as our passion to join the biker JayZ and Beyoncé scene began to diminish. We rarely mentioned it, and even when we did, it just wasn't the same. Soon we stopped talking about it entirely, the shared fantasy consumed by realistic practicalities and more urgent necessities.

But I remained fascinated with motorcycling.

I would see bikers on the road near our home, cruising in the beautiful weather of Southern California, and their rides seemed so exhilarating. These bikers looked so free and easy, supercool and confident, as if they had escaped the confinement of traditional motorists and embraced their freedom like a pouncing cheetah suddenly loosed from its cage.

I could shake the feeling no longer. I wanted in. I craved that kind of freedom to get away from it all. I read everything online I could find, compared bikes with different features, and their price tags. With my mind made up and due diligence completed, I headed off to shop at Harley-Davidson.

It didn't take me long to find and fall in love with my new bike, and soon she was in my garage waiting while I completed safety school and got my license. Learning to ride seemed to come naturally, and

I enjoyed it so much that I rode at least five days a week for the first few months. The experience felt just as incredible as I had envisioned.

Most bikers will tell you, it's one of the closest things to flying you'll ever do. I would find such freedom when I rode and felt very one with nature and with God. I would notice the beauty of my surroundings and take it all in. Beauty that you just don't get to see when you're enclosed in a car. When I rode my bike, my thoughts became clearer and more vivid. The entire experience seemed to cleanse my soul like nothing else. Riding became my thing. Everything was just what I expected and more—with one exception. My Beyoncé was missing.

Part of me started to feel guilty. There I was, having these wonderful experiences—ones changing my life, no doubt—but I was enjoying them alone. In a strange kind of way, it felt like somehow I was cheating on Sarah by having these experiences without her. She had said she was fine with my decision to bring my biker's dream to life, but she wasn't really interested in sharing it. Still, I figured there had to be a way.

So I began inviting her to accompany me, and she came out with me a few times. But I got the impression that while she enjoyed it, her experience wasn't as exhilarating as my own. I didn't want her to come along just to make me happy, and riding solo was easier. It was a more focused and freeing experience and became my favorite *me time* activity that I came to learn was important to my life.

Once I broke free from the guilt of being good to myself, I embraced the me time as a blessing, which made my rides even richer and more rewarding.

**Embrace your me time as a blessing.**

This experience also taught me a very valuable lesson, one that has revolutionized my thinking and positioned me for Balance like no other discipline: it taught me the crucial importance of unapologetic self-prioritization.

If you want to get to Balance, you must learn to never feel guilty about what it takes for you to get there.

## Selfish versus Self-ful

You've heard it before. Someone expressing frustration about others, with phrases like, "He is so full of himself!" or "All she thinks about is herself." Or maybe you've heard, "He thinks the whole world revolves around him."

We've all met a few people who rarely take into consideration anyone else when making decisions or consider the impact their choices will have on others. These types of personalities require a great amount of patience, and sometimes you even have to wonder if the mindset of "me, myself, and I" is the culprit behind many of the world's greatest problems. Their self-absorption illustrates what selfishness is. But there is an alternative mentality that places a great deal of emphasis on self, yet in a way that not only is critical for one's pursuit of Balance but also, as we will see, serves to benefit others in the greatest ways possible. It's what I call being self-ful.

What I'm referring to when I say self-ful is not the same thing as being full of self; it means to be mindful of self. Self-fulness takes self, its well-being, and its need for Balance into consideration first, and once self-equilibrium has been reached, attention is then given to others. This distinction may seem simple enough, but in practice being self-ful proves to be a challenge for the best of us.

I'll be the first to confess my struggle with practicing self-fulness. Let me give you an example. For the longest time, I've struggled with accepting the instructions we receive when traveling by plane concerning emergency procedures. You've heard it before: "Should the cabin lose pressure, oxygen masks will drop from the overhead compartment. Please place the mask over your own mouth and nose before assisting others."

So here's the thing. I'm a father who absolutely loves his children.

I mean, I would die for each one. Being told to serve myself oxygen first, in the event of an emergency, before attending to my loved ones still makes me cringe a little. Now, I understand the logic entirely and get that it makes all the sense in the world once you play the scenario out, but my initial tendency would be to put myself second.

We understand why the instruction is important. If you want to be in the best position to render aid to those you love, then you have to get what you need first so that you can bring your A game to the situation in order to save the ones you care about. It makes sense, and we have to not only learn the importance of responding this way but also wrap our mind around the virtue of putting self first.

The challenge is that somehow we have been programmed to believe that self prioritization is synonymous with selfishness, but this couldn't be farther from the truth. When we prioritize self and self finds Balance, everything around us flourishes. Although my wife doesn't always accompany me on my motorcycle adventures, she is highly supportive of my taking them. The version of me that she and my children receive when I walk back through that door after a soul-renewing cruise down the coast is more than worth what they gave up to afford me that time to myself. I'm more present with her and the kids. I seem to have unlimited patience when I return, and my happy spirit elevates the entire home. When I prioritize my need to live in Balance, everything connected to me seems to be aligned. In a way, prioritizing me is to prioritize the people and the things that are important to me.

## The Cost of Selflessness

There is another reason why prioritizing self is so important. Although being regarded as selfless can appear noble and commendable on the surface, it often becomes the reason why many well-meaning people end up bitter, resentful, and full of regret. Although acquiescing to others might offer the instant gratification of their approval, the long-term effects can be devastating. It's easy to withhold your voice in the name of avoiding conflict, but if you never speak up for yourself, you're not avoiding conflict. You are simply harboring that conflict within yourself. You become a ticking time bomb that will one day explode—or worse, implode.

A lifestyle of putting others before yourself not only can leave you extremely dissatisfied but is often symptomatic of low self-worth. If you don't love yourself first, you'll lose yourself, and many have lost themselves in the abyss of other people's needs, priorities, and expectations.

There's nothing worse than one day waking up and realizing that the life you have been living is not your own, and it happens more times than it should. So many people, believing they are being generously selfless, give their all for and to others at the expense of ultimately having nothing for themselves. Their lives become a tale of forsaken dreams and missed opportunities. They end up believing that they can never recover what they've sacrificed and become bitter, tormented by Night's narrative exacerbating their sense of irredeemable loss. Although this is a place we should aim to avoid by any means necessary, the good news is that even if we lose sight of being self-ful, if we can just get to Balance, the life we thought was lost forever still awaits us.

## Time to Get Away

Balance requires solitude—not just alone time but peaceful, uninterrupted, unplugged time for you to still your soul. It too is easier to accept as a concept than a regular, personal practice. Even when you make the time to get away to discover Balance, things can get a little tricky. We grow so accustomed to the relentless barrage of texts, news, headlines, celebrity updates, sales, new posts, and more on our phones that even when we unplug, we still struggle to find that peaceful place of solitude.

I've made it a priority to regularly take time away from work and all responsibilities, including family, to pursue and restore Balance, and I admit that each time is a struggle. I have a great deal of responsibility and am deeply invested in the organizations that I run, the businesses that I own, and the family that I love above it all. I'm engaged in leading in each of these arenas, regularly giving direction, support, and counsel. I sleep better at night knowing my hands are on the wheels of these important endeavors, and it can be tough to relinquish my grip, even when I know I've drifted away from Balance and need to correct my course.

I remember being away once and struggling to find the restful state that leads back to Balance. Instead of leaning into the opportunity for Balance, I found myself distracted and full of angst about what I had to temporarily leave behind to get there. Then something happened, and although it was years ago, I still remember it as if it happened moments ago. I heard a voice from another dimension—without question from the place of Balance—and it stated to me this simple phrase: *I've got that, I've got them, and I've got you. Rest!*

Immediately the weight lifted off me, and my soul was flooded with an overwhelming sense of peace. I leaned into the voice, which led me to Balance, and what I received and who I became when I got there was well worth letting go of my dedication to my responsibilities.

There is always an initial hesitation and a wrestling that takes place when I am being beckoned back toward Balance. I believe it's Night throwing everything it has at me to keep me from getting there, often cleverly using my imagination to trigger worst-case scenarios to distract me. I imagine that my family will fall apart during my absence as I pursue Balance. That my businesses will collapse without my hand on the wheel at all times. The truth, however, is that these areas rely on my doing what it takes to access the best version of myself, and there is nothing in the world that brings out my best like Balance.

Once I fight through Night's noisy lies and my own hesitation, having reassured myself of the important mission at hand, I relinquish the wheel, I let it all go, and I move forward toward the goodness that I know awaits me in the place of Balance. Almost immediately upon getting to my place of solitude, I experience an overwhelming awareness of how desperately this alone time was needed. A refreshing release comes over me, as if my soul had been longing for a reunion with its resting place and finally my body decided to grant its wish.

It's beyond cathartic. Something happens in a much deeper place, a homecoming of sorts, and when in that level of clarity, I vow to never again allow my soul to be separated from what I'm feeling. Although I know it's not that easy, I nevertheless come away from each of these Balance pursuits with a greater determination to do a better job of getting away from the constant noise of life—even the good noise of the people and things I love—in order to create more opportunities for this level of soul connection.

This connection is key. It allows you to tap into the rhythm of your soul, the beat of which is always choreographing your path to Balance if you will be still enough—and alone enough—to hear it. Self-fulness requires solitude.

## Beyond Self-Love

Commitment to solo time is one of the greatest evidences of self-love. It goes beyond self-love, however; it's self-*like*. Self-love is a term that became popular through movements in the fifties and sixties and was mostly about not feeling bad about pursuing your own happiness and advantages in life. This way of thinking was a drastic departure from some of the prevailing beliefs that suggested that being self-minded—or self-ful, as I like to call it—was evil, narcissistic, and arrogant. Thank God we've come a long way from such thinking, as even the mental health community sees the merit in self-love and believes it is a vital part of self-help.

But self-like is where the rubber meets the road. This goes beyond inspirational quotes on social media, T-shirts, and bumper stickers.

Nothing says you like yourself more than spending extended amounts of time with yourself—and learning to enjoy it.

Keep in mind, there is a difference between being alone and being lonely. Unfortunately, some people cannot distinguish between the two. The prevailing difference between being alone and being lonely is perspective. It's the difference between a mentality of abundance and one of scarcity. Loneliness approaches being alone from the perspective of deficit. Loneliness suggests that if I am by myself, I am somehow being deprived of something.

For some people it's the ultimate fear of missing out. They assume, whether or not they recognize it, that someone else is required in order to fulfill any experience, as opposed to regarding the company of another as an optional dynamic of self-experience. The healthiest perspective concerning being alone is to realize that as long as I am fully present with myself, I have everything I will ever need. It's an amazing space to arrive to. Aloneness is beautiful. There are some things that can be experienced only in solitude. The journey to Balance is one of them.

Have you ever had a solo experience that was absolutely wonderful, and then you try to recount it to another and it doesn't seem to have the impact on them as it did on you? Or have you experienced an amazing sunset that you could liken to your own private art show in the sky? You get excited and want your friends to experience it, so you take a photo, but the image just doesn't seem to capture the beauty the way you experienced it.

We tend to believe that everything is meant to be shared with others, but sometimes those unexpected special moments that happen to you are meant just for you. We all would get more out of these moments if we resisted the temptation to make them a group experience and rather learned to have solo parties from time to time and appreciate the beauty of inviting only ourselves to dance.

Finding Balance doesn't happen in groups. It's an individual pursuit, a solo mission, and if, for fear of loneliness, you avoid the alone times that your soul craves, you will miss the very environment that heals the mentality that causes you to feel lonely in the first place. Loneliness is evidence that Night has cast its shade upon you, and when the opportunity to take the solo trip to Balance presents itself, Night—for fear of being exposed—will casts it scariest shadows as a last attempt to disrupt your journey.

But remember what you learned in school about shadows. They appear only when light is present, which means Night is trying to hide something from you—perhaps the breakthrough your soul has been longing for. So stand up to loneliness, fight it, break through it, and get to the light so Balance can cause its sun to shine on the part of your being that is deceiving you and telling you that you, alone, are not enough.

## Afraid of Alone

You've likely heard it said before that the opposite of love is not hate but fear. I've found this to be true. Think about it. Love is affirming and inviting. It inspires confidence, freedom, and self-acceptance. Fear, on the other hand, is scary, inhibiting, and intimidating. It cultivates nervousness, second-guessing, limitation, and insecurity. Fear and love showcase the difference between Night and Day, and believe it or not, some people even have a fear of self, which is why they find it difficult to leave the crowd in order to find Balance.

For people who struggle with a fear of self, the notion of being by themselves, left with their own thoughts and facing only themselves, is terrifying. Night has convinced them life is safer when it's noisier. Fearing self is basically fearing the unknown within you. Will my experience with self reveal that I am a failure, an imposter, an outcast unworthy of the things that I desire in the dream for my life? Will the stillness of my soul reveal that they are out of reach? Will I find love in this intimate place of vulnerability, or will I discover the ultimate rejection—self-rejection? On a good day, I can shrug off or explain away the criticism and rejection of others, but where can I go if the real me rejects the me I've grown comfortable being?

This is an unspoken fear and dilemma for many people. If you dig deep enough, will you discover that you have at various times in your life experienced the fear of self? Deciding to stay busy at work, exhausting yourself with endless activities that distract you from being alone with yourself, leaving room only for bedtime and then waking up and starting over again? Perhaps it manifests itself in your desiring to be around others all the time, filling your life with companionship, sometimes even knowing it isn't the best company, but accepting anything to keep from being alone—with you.

I recall a time in my life shortly after I had left a long-term relationship. I was excited about my new start and all the possibilities life had for me, but I also knew that in addition to therapy I would need to do a lot of processing in order to move forward in a healthy way. Guess what? I had no problem seeing my therapist on a weekly basis but found it difficult to find the time to spend with myself.

In what I later came to discover was a bad case of self-avoidance, I began to fill up what should have been alone time with the company of others. Desperate to escape myself, I kept putting off the alone time I knew I needed and filled it with anything I could, from new friendships to dating and sometimes even hypocritically giving spiritual and self-help advice to others. In hindsight, I discovered that my fear of self is what created the real imposter. Only after experiencing the pain of ending two short-lived relationships that never should have begun in the first place did I accept that I could no longer postpone my solitude. If I wanted to move forward, I would have to push through, and that's exactly what I did. I overcame the fear, embraced my alone time, and experienced a life-changing series of breakthroughs that only Balance could have offered.

Admittedly, the fear of self is real, and it can be extremely intimidating, but you can't let it keep you from Balance. It's a daunting barrier, a wall of darkness within that we all must scale. But there is abundant light—and, I might add, abundant life—just on the other side. There's a you on the other side of that wall that is the you that you've been trying to be but couldn't access. It's the best you—the balanced you. So whatever you do, don't let the false fear of *you* rob you of that you!

# The Power of Solo

Night has done a fantastic job of selling us the idea that being solo is somehow a disadvantage. We are inundated with images of couples sharing romantic moments, families celebrating during the holidays, and of course the girls' trip to the exotic island with blue seas and tanned faces and everyone having the time of their lives. #BFF. #BestTimeEver.

There is beauty in each of those scenarios, without question. I've posted several images like that on the internet myself. But here's the thing: there is also unique beauty in solo moments—times that are difficult to capture in a social media post or to express in a tweet. And because of the power of media and imagery in the era we live in, the adage "Visibility is credibility" rings all too true. If you never see images that place value on solo moments, then solo moments must be insignificant.

But nothing could be farther from the truth.

Often the successes in love, relationships, and business that we gawk over are the byproduct of someone's solo time! What we don't consider is how many times the person who found amazing love spent solo time working on themselves, and as a result of becoming the best version of themselves were able to attract a mate at that same level, producing a happiness that far exceeded what they ever could have imagined. At other times, the entrepreneur whose accomplishment inspires you achieved their success through practicing the discipline of solo time and discovered it to be the place where their most revolutionary ideas and boundless creativity happens. Studies even suggest that there is a connection between a healthy amount of alone time and self-awareness, and as we know, self-aware people tend to be high achievers in the areas that matter most—relationships, work, business, and overall happiness.

Many of my greatest moments—indelible moments that would define my life forever—happened during planned solo experiences. I've received breakthrough insight and clarity about my work, purpose, marriage, even wisdom on how to navigate challenging situations with family or in a business deal. There has never been a time when I didn't come away from a long motorcycle ride, a stroll on the beach, or a walk in the park better than when I went into it.

Now, to be clear, on the way to any solo experience, you will always feel the resistance of Night.

Night is afraid of the light of Balance that we encounter during moments of intentional solo time. Night would rather keep our lives noisy, crowded, distracted, and restricted. Night loves the rat race and wants to keep us on the hamster wheel lest we break, meditate, and get the epiphany that although we may be busy, we aren't balanced. Arriving at Balance requires focus and single-mindedness. This is unattainable in the noise. The noise of busyness, as well as the busyness itself, creates roadblocks to Balance.

Noise and Night work hand and hand. They both keep us from being present to ourselves. The same way Night diminishes our ability to see, noise diminishes our ability to perceive. When our life is crowded and noisy, it is difficult to perceive and analyze our own thoughts. Without the vital process of solo time, we easily end up stuck in our ruts and just drift through life unable to ensure that the life we're living is our own, let alone the best possible one. Fears and frustrations, ego and insecurity can hide in the noise. The crowd is a cloak for dysfunction, and until you yield to Balance's wooing toward solo time, you will experience far less than what is possible. And the saddest loss of all is that you might not recognize it.

## The I-Team

You've probably heard the popular saying "There's no I in team." I get that. When you're a part of a team, you have to consider the team and do what's best for the sake of the team. You sacrifice your needs and wants for the greater good.

This is a noble concept but not without its flaws. If you overlook the singularity of self and fail to know it well enough to master it, then you will ultimately do a disservice to the team. We owe it to the teams of our lives—our spouses, our children, our friends, our coworkers, our business partners, our investors, and even strangers we encounter—not to be satisfied with simply being a part of the whole. We owe it to them and to ourselves to do what it takes to offer the best version of ourselves possible.

We must see solo time not as a crime against those we love but rather as a gift to them. When solo time is done right, we'll return to them better, more patient, empathetic, and conscientious. We'll have more clarity, wisdom, and innovative thoughts to move things forward. Balance always brings out our divine virtues. May we forever overcome Night's intimidating narrative about facing ourselves alone and embrace the spirit of optimistic curiosity about the version of ourselves we get to discover when we silence the noisiness of life.

> ## Balance always brings out our divine virtues.

Make no mistake about it, the best you is the balanced you, and self-prioritization is a critical step. Solo time is everything.

Throughout our journey together we are going to discover many practical steps that will aid us in achieving Balance. We are just scratching the surface when it comes to understanding the fullness of what Balance is and the steps that it takes to get there, but your commitment to alone time is fundamental to the process. For this reason, before we move on to understanding more about Balance, I'd like you to make not only a commitment to but a plan for regularly scheduled alone times.

I'd like you to put them on your calendar, as you would any other meeting. Then, next to the solo time appointment, I want you to write down your why. What do you expect to gain during that time? What do you need most right now? Clarity, courage, affirmation, fresh creativity, wisdom, inspiration, happiness, wholeness, all the above? It's important that we remind ourselves of the reason we are doing the things that we know Night and busyness will oppose. It's a war, and we must create advantages for ourselves at every turn.

Knowing what I know now about self-prioritization and the impact it has on the things that matter most to us, I wonder if the scene of those two bikers riding off into the sunset had more symbolism than I thought. What if the scene I was witnessing of the two of them riding in perfect harmony was the culmination of two solo rides that in time merged together beautifully after each rider experienced Balance—on their own.

# CHAPTER 3

---

# What the Soul Craves

*One can choose to go back toward safety or forward toward growth.*

—ABRAHAM MASLOW

There was a time when I knew I needed to get away for some alone time, but I ended up dragging my feet, putting it off for weeks and weeks because I was too busy. I was CEO of two sizable nonprofit organizations, and I was right in the middle of moving my private businesses forward, including the close of a major real estate deal. Although I needed a getaway, feeling the urge deep down, my business responsibilities and opportunities caused me to override my internal longing. Soon it felt like my wheels were spinning in place as I kept procrastinating about pursuing what I needed most.

During this time, I began to notice that my best was slipping away from me. My patience was disappearing, my thought life began to decline, and the adrenaline fueling my actions began to run out. My memory started slipping, and if I am to be honest, my sharpness and innovation started to trend downward.

On top of all this, I had a book to write—this very book you're reading—with a pressing deadline, and I had next to nothing to pour into a new literary work. The pressure mounting and my back now against the wall, I finally booked a trip for some away time. I had run out of excuses. Not getting what I needed at the deepest level had become irresponsibility, not only to myself but to the businesses and the people I wanted to protect by staying engaged.

I didn't like the me I was becoming.

I was long overdue, so I made the decision to go.

Before it was too late.

## Needs Must

Looking back, I can see that I needed that time away to get back to Balance. And when I use the word *needed* here, I mean I needed to get away and regain my internal equilibrium as much as I needed to breathe, eat, and sleep. Now, I realize this kind of need may strike you more as a luxury.

"Touré, I can't afford to take time off and just go stare at the horizon somewhere. I've got bills to pay and kids to feed and people counting on me." I hear you, my friend. But I must also remind you that the most important person you have counting on you is *you*. Remember, you need to put your soul needs first in order to serve, love, and give to those around you from your place of Balance.

There's an old phrase, "needs must," that I heard older people say when I was growing up. I wasn't sure exactly what they meant until I was nearly an adult, and then it became clear. "Needs must" refers to those things that have to be done whether you feel like it or not. They may be unpleasant or undesirable, uncomfortable or unfavorable, but circumstances often dictate what needs *must* be addressed.

I gained insight on "needs must" when I learned about the late American psychologist Abraham Maslow, best known for an idea he proposed in the journal *Psychological Review* in 1943. In this article, he introduced what is now known as Maslow's hierarchy of needs.

Although Maslow admitted at the time that there was little scientific evidence for his theory, scholars later came to agree that humanity undeniably has universal needs. Yet the ranking of those needs remains the subject of much debate.

Maslow's five-tiered, pyramid-shaped graph had the five human needs broken down into three sections: basic needs, psychological needs, and self-fulfillment needs. The basic needs section included physiological needs like food and water. Next up the pyramid were safety needs, and continuing up was the need for love and belonging. This was followed by the human need for esteem, which included feelings of accomplishment and prestige. And at the top of Maslow's pyramid was the need for self-actualization, which involved achieving one's full potential and included the need for creative endeavors and meaningful activities.[5]

When I consider Maslow's theory, I see both the profundity of his observations and the problematic nature of generalization. I do believe, however, that he was onto something. Perhaps something beyond what he understood or was permitted to fully articulate. Let me try to explain. If we remove from his graph the basic physical needs (food, water, security), we're left with fundamental intangibles that the vast majority, if not every human being, craves. Intangibles such as experiencing love, a place of belonging, a sense of value, productivity, and accomplishment. I don't know anyone who doesn't desire most of these, including you, I suspect.

What's also interesting about Maslow's theory is that the human needs he described are aligned with some of the deeper cravings of our soul. And if we are able to discern these longings and learn to respond appropriately, they will lead us right into the ever-present light of Balance. There's a longing for equilibrium in us all, a hunger for the nourishment we find in Balance, and until it is identified and fulfilled, we will remain frustrated and prohibited from exploring and maximizing key areas of our lives.

Finding and sustaining Balance requires that we discover the diet that the highest version of ourselves craves. There's a you in you who gets you and understands who you truly are and what you need in order to become that you. That's the you who wants more for you than the lesser you would allow you to desire and pursue.

This is why sometimes you will feel unsettled and may not have an explanation for how or what you feel. Everything can look fine on paper, but deep down you will sense that something is missing. The worst thing any of us can do is ignore that unsettling. There is an opportunity in it. Discomfort is very often an opportunity for growth, healing, and progress if we would just learn to listen to it, discern what it's trying to tell us, and respond accordingly.

## Reunion with Your Soul

You will recall that we've established soul-awareness as the highest form of self-awareness. Our soul is the most honest and authentic version of ourselves, not to be mistaken with the highest version of ourselves. It's not our greatest self but positions us to access that version of ourselves through our ability to listen to our soul's guidance toward the state of Balance.

Remember, your soul is always after something. It doesn't lay dormant or inactive. It perpetually thirsts and longs for that which only Balance can supply. It longs to be settled, to find its peace, affirmation, wisdom, and creativity and for the limitations that hinder you to be removed. Discovering Balance requires a certain sensitivity to and awareness of the soul and what it is longing for at any given moment in time. It takes practice and self-awareness to listen and take your soul's longings seriously.

When I finally listened to my soul's deep insistence for solitude during that season of busyness, I found the kind of rest and comfort that comes only from Balance. My beachside getaway was about a ninety-minute drive from home, and as soon as I walked into my accommodations, I felt a familiar presence greet me. Usually when I first enter a new environment where I am to stay, I walk through the entirety of that place, saying a prayer to dispel any negative energy or lingering spirit left over from previous inhabitants and events. I then welcome the spirit of Balance—the unique personality who permeates the realm of Balance—into the atmosphere.

This time, however, it was different. The moment I walked into the room, I could sense that the spirit of Balance was there already, waiting for me like an old friend. It was like a homecoming I didn't even realize I needed, and it created the opportunity to regain perspective concerning my life, my priorities, and my relationships.

Within minutes upon my arrival, I kneeled to pray, surrendering myself to the moment and looking forward to the transformation that the alone time would afford me. Then something happened I had never experienced before. As I opened my mouth to utter words of adoration and gratitude, a part of me emerged from a place much deeper than the consciousness of my mind and gave intense expression to what it had been feeling beneath the surface for some time.

The best way for me to describe it is this: Picture the most emotional reunion between two people that you can imagine. Envision the reunion between a solider and their spouse after spending years apart, the soldier having left for an indefinite period of time, not to mention the uncertainty of the soldier's fate when they go away to war. Imagine the overwhelming joy the two would experience when the solider unexpectedly walks through the door. The relief, the reconnection, the reunion.

Or perhaps it was like when a loved one suffers an injury and slips into a coma for a very long time. Imagine visiting that loved one for months and months with little to no signs of progress, and then one day to your surprise this loved one awakes from their sleep, fully engaged as they reenter consciousness. Once again the relief, the reconnection, the reunion.

I cried out from a part of me that I don't remember accessing much before that day. It was my soul, and being reacquainted with

Balance, it wept and leapt for joy as if a long-lost companion had been rediscovered. It was bliss like never before, and in that moment everything changed. Things that I had been worried and stressed about didn't matter anymore. Peace washed over me, assuring me in the most certain way that all was well and that the only thing that mattered in that moment was the moment itself. My highest self emerged; a version of myself that I hadn't seen in a long time stood up in that encounter. All fear and angst evaporated, and I had a divine clarity about everything, especially my work, businesses, and family. I was aligned with the rhythm of this place of Balance, and everything was bright.

Things that were once problems were no longer obstacles but became opportunities for me to exercise newfound creativity to resolve. The wisdom and innovation I discovered in Balance proved to be limitless. From this place of rest, I could see my way forward in every area so clearly. I could see all the ways that the imbalanced version of me was stifling my greatness and progress. There was no Night, only the warmth and light and clarity of Day. I remember thinking that I never wanted this perfect alignment with Balance and the profound consciousness that came with it to end.

So when it was finally time to return, I packed and prepared to go home, but before I left, I felt I had to do something. I walked to the spot where I knelt when I first arrived, and I made a promise to my soul. The promise: that I would never get that far away from Balance again. It hasn't always been easy, but so far I've kept that promise.

I had nourished my soul with the fruit of Balance.

## Barriers to Soul-Awareness

Ever since that life-changing soul encounter I had during my getaway, I've been committed to championing the call for everyone to be not just self-aware but soul-aware. And as a result, I'm often asked for directions.

Now, I must admit up front that the path to Balance is unique to the individual, and the soul's instruction for guidance to get there will adjust to meet the needs of the individual at a given moment. In the case of my time away to achieve Balance, I needed to be in a specific environment. I had options on resorts to go to; however, the only place that I had a deep inner peace about spending the time at was the place I decided, or better yet *was led*, to go to. There are other times when I'm drawn to do something different. Sometimes what gets me to Balance is to take a motorcycle ride down the coast or through the canyons. It varies moment by moment, but what is always consistent is the state of rest that awaits me when I yield to what I discern that my soul desires.

The leading of the soul is not the challenging part. Once you identify it, discerning its promptings with time and discipline becomes part of your spiritual routine. Getting to the soul, however, is the tricky part because certain obstacles will always stand in your way. Let's consider some of them now.

Although I mentioned noise previously, I cannot overemphasize the way it drowns out the voice of your soul. The loud cacophony of voices, both external and internal, do not have volume control unless you take ownership and create one for yourself. And perhaps the more challenging of the two is the noise inside your mind.

Our personal thought life can be a world all to itself. We have thoughts that we are consciously thinking as well as thoughts that play out in our subconscious minds. Then you add to that the external noise that comes in the form of the thoughts and words of others. With the advance of technology, we are inundated with perspectives and opinions all the time. We don't even have to leave home to be exposed to them. Sometimes the external noise is so overwhelming and dominating that we can't decipher between our thoughts and the thoughts of others.

Then add to that soundtrack any negative thoughts we may have which add additional layers of noise to our thought life. Worry and fear are loud and dominating noises that consume an exorbitant amount of energy and focus. More noise. And let us not forget about busyness. Our calendars are filled with activities and events that keep us going nonstop. There is often the illusion that busyness is the same as productivity, but studies have shown that this is not the case. Some people are embracing the discipline of "non-time" to help them get a handle on the noisiness of life.

If you're wondering about non-time, author and TED speaker Steven Kotler coined this term for the quiet time alone that is uniquely yours, a block of time when you are insulated from the world's noise and demands. For Kotler, each morning between 4:00 a.m. and 7:30 a.m. provides "a vast stretch of emptiness" for him to recharge creatively.[6] Although I suspect Kotler may still need getaways, he finds a way to sustain Balance by carving out this time each day in which he can escape adversarial noise and demanding disruptions.

**The person who will find Balance must learn the discipline of regularly muting life's noise.**

The person who will find Balance must learn the discipline of regularly muting life's noise. Employing effective ways of quieting our lives will allow us to tap into the rhythm of the soul which leads us into Balance.

Although I can't overemphasize the importance of physically removing yourself from the hustle and bustle, physical escape for rest and recovery of Balance does not necessarily mean that your mind and heart will follow suit. It is quite possible to escape the busyness physically but not silence the noise, and thereby the gift made possible by the alone time is forfeited. On the other hand, sometimes the luxury of escaping our environment in a physical way is simply not possible. That's why it's important to regularly find time mentally, emotionally, and spiritually to eliminate noise and maintain Balance.

It doesn't have to be early in the morning, like Mr. Kotler's, nor does it need to be every day. But it should be an exercise you cultivate if you want to feed your soul what it needs most.

## All One Is Never Alone

The best way to describe what needs to happen in order to escape life's noise to achieve Balance is to look more closely at the term *alone*. Isn't it interesting how even seeing *alone* causes our minds to immediately go to the negative? How many times have you been out on a date or with friends and noticed someone who was by themselves and thought, "Oh, that poor thing, over there all by themselves." Sometimes you may even wonder if you should approach them and strike up a conversation or invite them into your circle of community to deliver them from their deprived state of aloneness. If that's ever been you or you know that your extrovert personality possesses that tendency, before you give in to that thought or make that move, I want you to remember what I'm getting ready to share with you.

The term that we use today for *alone* originated from the Middle English phrase *all ana*, which—watch this—never places its emphasis on a person being by themselves. That's not what this phrase meant. The phrase *all ana* literally means "wholly oneself," and most accurately "all one." What a huge difference!

The goal in silencing the noisiness of life, whether you do so by physically being by yourself or by finding a way to detach from the noise mentally, is to become all one—wholly oneself. Noise divides us and fragments our identities and passions. When life is noisy and crowded, we can hardly do anything to its full potential. Any great person will tell you that greatness requires relentless focus and the ability to subdue the noisiness of life. Why? Because this allows you to be fully yourself. To sense your soul's voice and hear its needs, you will need to remove every sound around you, quieting all of the external and internal noise so that you can perceive your path to Balance.

# Breath of Fresh Balance

Whether you go away to find this quiet or develop the discipline of blocking out the noise, meditation is a vital part of the Balance diet. Although there are many forms of meditation, the goal should always be to bring you to the state of *all ana*—all one. My practice in doing so is to start by breathing deeply and intentionally. The one thing about breathing is that you can do it anytime and anywhere. Of course, the ideal way to meditate is to have a place (or places) set aside for this special time, but again sometimes you have to get what you need on the fly. As long as you get to breathe—all of yourself, not just your body—then you're moving in the right direction.

The first thing I do while focusing on my breathing is to release it all. When I say all, I mean *all*—the joyful along with discordant noise. Remember, the good noise is connected to our relationships with our loved ones, noble responsibilities, current successes, exciting opportunities, and our purpose in life. Breathing as part of meditation helps us center ourselves, refusing to be swayed by either excitement or confusion. We're balancing ourselves so that we can eventually live in the state of Balance.

When I'm starting to focus on my breathing, my exhale will be much deeper than my inhale because I'm letting go of all the noise, stress, and constraints. When I inhale, I'm taking in the state of rest. In my mind I am repeating the phrase "I have no lack." In through my nose, out through my mouth with my lips pursed as if I am gently blowing out a candle. I continue this process for as long as it takes me to find center. I know when I'm there, because a very filling peace will come over me, and that's when I feel connected to my soul's rhythm. From there emerges insight, divine guidance, and unlimited creativity. I'm balanced and there's nothing like it.

There are times when the process isn't as smooth and seamless as I would desire. Sometimes the noisy chatter is relentless. This is when the practice of mindfulness must be turned up in a greater way.

Mindfulness, like meditation, has many definitions and approaches, depending on who you ask. For me, mindfulness is about *minding* what I am minding. It is paying attention to the things that are accessing my mind at a given point in time. Anyone who is going to do well in life must become someone who guards their thoughts, what I call a thought regulator in my previous book, *Wholeness*.

You and I have a responsibility to qualify every thought that takes up space in the precious real estate of our mind. Our mind is a place only for real and productive things. Things that are true, optimistic, and hopeful. Our mind cannot be the Wild, Wild West, where anything and everything comes and goes.

You have more say over what you think than you realize, and being mindful of what you are minding is paramount. This is a discipline that is developed over time, but you can and will become a thought regulator. One rule that I have as it relates to what I will allow myself to mind is this: if the thought doesn't serve me, affirm the best in me, or lead me to Balance, it isn't worthy of me.

Sometimes the noise fragmenting us is playing itself out not in our conscious mind but in our unconscious mind. The conscious mind is the part that you are aware of. This is the place where you think, plan, process, and experience emotions. The unconscious mind consists of processes of the mind that happen automatically. It's on cruise control, operates outside our awareness, and is a huge determinant of behavior.

When the noise hindering and distracting you is hidden in the unconscious, it often requires more work, but you can still overcome it. In addition to the obvious and effective tool of professional therapy with a counselor, one way to uncover the noise that plagues you unconsciously is to pay attention to your feelings and actions. They are telling a story, and often when you discover that story, you'll find the source of the noise murmuring in your unconscious mind.

Just because this story is emerging from your subconscious doesn't mean you can't pinpoint it eventually. Study your behavior. Write down your feelings. Courageously explore yourself and talk to someone you trust. During this process, fill your conscious mind with correlating truths until your behavior is driven by the new thoughts that you have determined to think upon, believe, and consequently experience. The goal of it all, in the task of meditation, is to bring all of yourself into focusing on one thing—perceiving your soul and its promptings toward Balance.

## Proud and Powerless

There's something else I'd like to point out that often impedes soul-awareness: pride. I'm not talking about pride in the sense of an arrogant aloofness that turns its nose up in superiority to what it perceives as less-than-worthy things. This pride is different, subtle, and often born out of good and noble intentions.

The pride that I am referring to is expressed by the need to always be on top of things, to be in control of everything. No matter how tragic or perplexing what you are experiencing may be, you are locked into the default setting that consistently uses phrases like "I'm fine," "I'm okay," "It's all good," and "I've got this." This type of pride results from believing that the greatest existential threat to a person's life is to not be in control of it.

Now, I can certainly empathize with such a way of being. After all, life can be extremely challenging. None of us gets to escape reality. And in order to win at life, it takes a certain fortitude and mental toughness to face whatever life brings our way. There's something to be said about not allowing your circumstances to dominate your life and diminish your will to live. Nothing should be given that power.

While I wholeheartedly subscribe to the idea of not letting life kick your butt, sometimes it does, not permanently but seasonally, and in those moments it's okay to say, "Ouch," "This hurts," or to use phrases that are on the forbidden list of the proud, such as, "I need help."

There is a difference between being determined to overcome something and failing to acknowledge the overwhelming, confusing, painful reality of that situation. Failing to acknowledge the truth of a situation is dishonest and distances us from connection with our soul. In the case of my constantly delaying the time away that I knew I needed, I was dishonoring the hunger of my soul for soul care. I was starving for Balance but kept gorging on busyness.

To live with the assumption that we're fine and everything is under control is more often the precursor for defeat than is our acknowledgment that we are in trouble. To properly care for our souls, we must acknowledge that they need care and feeding. Our routine trips to our physician or dentist acknowledge our commitment to our physical health. Why, then, do we allow our spiritual health to decline, or feel it is unworthy of the same focused attention and remediation? The true nature of our soul doesn't perceive our honesty as weakness, any more than a doctor perceives our describing our symptoms as fragility. It is in the agreement between the truth and the soul's recognition of what it takes to get us from there to Balance that the breakthrough—not the breakdown—begins.

# Fake Food

The last barrier to soul-awareness comes in the form of things we often fill our lives with in an attempt to drown out the noise and satisfy our soul's hunger. Rather than turning to the solution of alone time and brokenness to discover and feed the true needs of the soul, we often choose shortcuts and cheap imitations that temporarily mimic satisfaction for the soul. It's not even fast food; it's fake food! The usual suspects include unhealthy relationships, people pleasing, risqué images on social media for thirst of validation, alcohol, drug and sex addiction, overspending to keep up a false image, clout chasing, and the list goes on and on and on.

I cast no judgment, because many of us have been seduced into considering, if not full-on engaging in, these destructive distractions—particularly those who aren't yet self-aware, let alone soul-aware. I can clearly see how so many can easily fall into these traps. Night is diligent to make sure that these things are always within reach. This unprofitable fruit hangs low on trees all around us and requires far less effort and focus than the disciplines that lead to the soul-awareness we've been discussing.

These counterfeit remedies to the cry of the soul are often accepted—and even promoted—in our world. Dysfunction is on display at every turn, often marketed at the highest level. It's all fun and games and freedom of individual expression until the harmful fruit of such a lifestyle can no longer be ignored or denied. Headlines tell the tale of overdoses, painful breakups, mental breakdowns, and all of the evidences that prove that if we don't deal with the needs of our soul, our avoidance to do so will deal with us.

Another thing to consider when it comes to our tendency toward these counterfeit healings is that although they may temporarily drown out life's noise, they also drown out our soul's cry, making it all the more difficult to pinpoint our true place of need. This in turn makes the needs of our soul greater and all the more desperate. Hunger ignored becomes malnutrition in the soul as it does in the body.

I'd like to offer this discipline to you or anyone you may know who struggles with attempting to cover up a soul cry with counterfeit solutions. This exercise is not to take the place of therapy, recovery programs, or the myriad of paths to inner healing that, thank God, are available to those who desire help. This rather is a powerful personal tool that will help you to quiet the noise and counter the counterfeits. If you want to pierce through the manifold layers of noise and levels of false breakthroughs that keep you from the still, small voice of your soul, then perhaps nothing is more effective than fasting.

## Lasting by Fasting

Essentially, what it means to fast, in this context, is to deprive ourselves of the things we've crowded into our hearts, minds, and bodies in an effort to address our soul's hunger. Fasting—from too much of anything, really—draws a line in the sand and requires us to be honest about our pain and brokenness, not to mention being truthful with ourselves about the counterfeits we've settled for instead of the soul food we crave. Because let's be honest, any reprieve that comes our way through the counterfeit is at best only temporary. It's like a black hole that needs to be fed but is never fully satisfied. That's not healing and prolongs and even complicates the inevitable: a face-to-face meeting with your soul. It's going to happen one way or another because, as Jesus once implied, *you can't exchange anything for your soul.*[7] Your soul is priceless, cannot be discarded or disregarded, and holds the keys to Balance.

In the place of clarity and with a made up mind, the person willing to fast will make an agreement with themselves that they're doing the hard work of saying no to the substitute, in pursuit of the real thing. I've learned that the problem with a false healing is that it occupies the space designated for a real one. If I try to create Balance on my own superficial terms, then I'm stuck with only that which I can create for myself. Not to mention it is the lesser version of me doing the creating.

But fasting is more than just saying no to the unprofitable; it's about saying yes to a process. One that requires replacing the pursuit of the placebo with the quest for truth and self-discovery, no matter how challenging it gets. Knowing the truth and becoming intimately involved with the truth will set you free. Do the work, attend the session, attend the service, read the book, and don't forget to pray.

Balance is cheering for you, and your soul is awaiting your cooperation. There is more working for you than you know—so

> Fasting is more than just saying no to the unprofitable; it's about saying yes to a process.

much more than what is working against you. Light will always be greater than even the darkest Night. Fasting from what you've used to falsely fill your inner hunger won't be easy. Remember, it is a radical shift from the norms you've grown accustomed to. It will not happen automatically. You will have to be intentional and set up some accountability.

When I say accountability, I don't mean engaging a self-righteous and harsh individual who motivates with fear and put-downs. I'm thinking more along the lines of an encourager. I like to call these special people destiny advocates. They are convinced concerning who you are. They are for you and always speak up to you and never down. They call you by your real name and won't allow you to settle into any identity that is less than who you are.

These people should be the first people you want to call and share your most exciting news with. There should be so much trust in the relationship that they also are the first ones you want to call when your world seems to be falling apart—even by your own hands. Perhaps you have to think about that for a while to discover who might be worthy. That's understandable, but don't delay too long when you're committed to begin fasting. Believe me, it makes a world of difference to have someone cheer you on in your journey and, like a good dietician or nutritionist, remind you what you really need for soul satisfaction. They will be there with you in your moment of victory, when you get free from the barriers that have kept you from partnering with your soul and realizing Balance.

The diet that your soul craves grows in the gardens of Balance. We're going even farther into the process in the next chapter, but before you turn this page, my prayer is that the faint cry of your soul would be perceived by you and known like never before in your life. That you would be courageous enough to work the disciplines and practices that will create the type of stillness that gives you access to your soul's voice. I also pray that every counterfeit behavior, activity, or tendency that would masquerade as fulfillment would be exposed and disposed of. I ask that you feel your soul's permission to be vulnerable in healthy brokenness so that the breakthrough and blessing of Balance can afford you its gifts beyond what you even know you need. Amen.

# CHAPTER 4

# The Gift of Rest

*Each person deserves a day away in which no problems are confronted, no solutions searched for. Each of us needs to withdraw from the cares which will not withdraw from us.*

—MAYA ANGELOU

Everything great that has ever happened to me in life occurred when I somehow found myself in the place of rest. I mean *everything*, from book deals to viral teaching messages, entertainment and business opportunities, even meeting and marrying the love of my life. It all happened when I entered the space of rest.

Now I think it's important for me to define what I mean by rest, because it may not be what you're thinking. The rest that I am referring to isn't how we feel after we take a nap or get a good night's sleep. It's not even how we feel after we return from a much-needed vacation or getaway. This rest is something entirely different; it's a consciousness. This rest is about a marvelous, unique state of being created by an awareness that too few people get to experience. This rest may be one of the greatest gifts that Balance affords us.

What makes this state so amazing is not simply what is there. The most incredible part about this rest is what *is not*. This state of rest is devoid of all conflict, preoccupation, fear, angst, longing, need, or lack. There's nothing missing, nothing to be desired; it's completeness. This awareness accepts that everything needed is present, and therefore whoever enters into this state goes from confusion to clarity, from emptiness to fullness, from not enough to more than enough, and from desiring to having. When this rest state is realized, since everything is already present in it, all we need to do is posture ourselves for receiving.

## Fishing Lessons

This state of rest reminds me of a story in the New Testament about a fisherman who had been at sea all night and into the next morning trying to catch fish. His efforts failed miserably, and the story emphasizes how the fisherman had been going at it—laboriously all night, albeit unsuccessfully. He literally caught *nothing*. The man then has an encounter with Jesus, who distracts him from his fishing failure by enlisting his nautical services to help him do a good deed. Once that mission is complete, Jesus tells the fisherman to let down his net. When he does, to his surprise it begins to fill with fish, and a lot of them. As he brings his net up, he sees more fish than he can count. His net begins to break because of the weight of the catch, requiring more nets because of this unimaginable haul.

With one shift the fisherman went from being exhausted, defeated, and unproductive to being inspired, amazed, reinvigorated, and successful. What he'd been looking for and more had been there all along. His successful catch took place in the same sea in which he had toiled all night, in the same boat, and with his same tools. So why was there such a different outcome? I believe the answer was rest. The state of rest, induced by his encounter with Jesus, was confirmation that the man had found Balance.

Jesus inviting the fisherman into service for a greater and divine good moved the frustrated man from a scarcity, or lack, mentality into what I like to call an abundance mentality. Once he was relieved of his preoccupation with toiling and trying to make something happen, he was inadvertently positioned for the abundance that had been there the entire time. Surely, the same number of fish were in the sea all along. But once the toiling mentality disappeared, giving way to the *have-already* consciousness, the fisherman could relax in the security of rest. He likely didn't recognize the shift when it happened, but he certainly experienced the joy of virtually effortless receiving.

So often we are just like this fisherman. If we aren't successful at achieving our goals, we assume that the way forward is to work harder. Balance, however, affords us a divine rest that stills the demanding waves of toil, conflict, and the lack mentality, placing us in the position to receive everything that already exists for us. In Balance, the place of rest, all of the resources associated with the fullness of our lives are abundant. We simply have to cast our nets.

## The Deficit Mentality

Most of us approach life and the things we desire from a deficit perspective. We pursue what we want, often aggressively and with the subconscious belief that whatever we are after is something we do not have, and must possess. We are often celebrated for how hard we work to accomplish our goals and are lauded for our tenaciousness along the way. I believe that hard work and tenacity are vital traits and that anyone who will achieve great things will embody such things; however, even in hard work there is a greater perspective. We don't work hard to get what we do not have; we work hard because what we are after is there already, just waiting to be possessed. Do you see the difference?

If I pursue my goal from the place of deficit, I won't be able to bring all of myself into the pursuit. The lack mentality is debilitating, and although many have achieved noteworthy things with such a disposition, it did not come without a steep price. Take the individual who grew up poor as a child, for instance. They may have memories of what appears to them as not having enough. They become adults and decide that they will never experience such deprivation again. Their fear of poverty drives them and they work hard—achingly hard. And they become successful, often very successful.

Now, here you may be thinking, "What's the problem? What's wrong with being successful? Especially *very* successful? How could being successful ever be a miss?" Those are fair questions. But the success part isn't the problem. The fear that's in the driver's seat is the problem.

There's a worthy and very interesting debate in the world about whether fear serves us or hinders us. The argument for fear is that it warns of danger, heightens our senses, and gives us an opportunity to protect ourselves, defend ourselves, or remove ourselves from danger. Some say fear provides us with an opportunity to demonstrate the virtue of courage, the brave act of advancing while danger is imminent. While I certainly agree with the importance of perceiving actual threats and being our best to handle dangerous situations, I believe that a consistent, driving fear ultimately works against us more than for us.

Why? Because fear accosts our imagination. It repeatedly puts our mind in overdrive by filling it with negative thoughts, worst-case outcomes, and disastrous possibilities, which studies show are more taxing on the psyche than positive ponderings. Not only does thinking positively put us in a better and more productive mood, but it is important to the health of our brain. Researchers at University College London say they have found that repetitive negative thinking is linked to cognitive decline, a higher number of harmful protein deposits in the brain, and as a result, a greater risk of dementia.[8]

So even if you do escape the typical byproducts of fear, which include attracting what you are afraid of—stagnation, procrastination, and diminished performance—and then go on to do great things, you discover strings attached, not only in the long term but every step along the way.

# Fear-Based Decisions

Decisions are powerful things. They chart the course of our lives. They are often threads that come together to form the tapestry of our future. Decisions are nothing to take lightly, especially important ones. In moments of decision, we need the freedom to bring all of ourselves to the table of consideration.

When we bring fear to the table, it restricts what is possible for us, because it filters the moment with negativity, resulting in a deficit mentality that puts us on the defense, aiming to preserve rather than prosper. Fear makes us forget that a decision is an opportunity for progress. It's a vital juncture, one that—if we choose well—can set us up for our best and brightest days. On the other side of a right decision could be everything we have ever prayed to receive.

Fear in the decision making process is a different story. It doesn't allow us to choose well, because of its preoccupation with trouble. It distracts us from the positive possibilities and brings a lesser version of ourselves to the moment of decision. You and I will never make the best decision if it is founded in fear. Anytime fear is driving your life, your potential for success will be capped.

Can you imagine a company becoming successful by building its business model around a fear of what their competition might do, instead of leveraging their own vision, talent, skill set, and uniqueness to drive the company forward into the future they've envisioned? Of course not; it would fail. No business is created based on what their competitor *might* do. The opportunity in front of them is the focus, not the what-ifs of fear. From the onset, the new business is forged in optimism about the possibilities of what could be achieved and the problems it intends to solve.

There will always be loss when fear drives anything. A preoccupation with failure stifles the creativity and innovation needed to succeed. The fear of not having enough may swell your bank account temporarily, but it will likely cost you a healthy relationship with your friends and family, because you were never present to participate in the moments that truly matter in life. If you're running a business, the fear of falling to competition could make you compromise the values you began with, costing you dearly in the long run. When values go out the window, morale slips, the work environment suffers, and the hope for sustained productivity disappears.

Fear is a part of Night's arsenal, and Night wants to keep you from Balance. What you fear becomes your master. It controls and manipulates you. Unless you do something about it, you will never escape it. It will haunt you and threaten you at every turn. Even when you achieve success, you can't enjoy it fully, because the fear driving your deficit mentality says, "It's still not enough. It's gonna run out. There's no time to take in the moment"—insert the sound of a whip cracking twice—"so get back to work!" So off we go, living not our best lives but greatly diminished ones at best.

In my previous book, *Wholeness,* I wrote a section in chapter 10 called "The Boogeyman Who Never Comes," in which I describe it this way: "It's the threat of what might happen that leaves you afraid of *what if* and prevents you from enjoying the blessings of *what is.* You become so preoccupied with wondering whether you are going to make it that you fail to consider that you *are* making it."[9]

Can you relate? Could a deficit mentality be sabotaging your happiness right now? Are you missing out on enjoying the moment you are in, because you have an internal taskmaster telling you it's not enough—or even worse, *you* are not enough? Is there possibly enough evidence in your life right now to assure you that you're on the right track and that things will go well for you? Or is there a fear-based lie chasing you right now, and if so, what is it? It is critical to recognize which thoughts are at the root of your fears, so that you can address them—head-on with the truth.

One all too common cause of these self-defeating mentalities is a past experience that didn't go the way you expected. Perhaps there's a memory of a painful breakup or a failed business venture. Maybe you remember being poor as a child and not having some of the things your classmates had. If we don't interpret our experiences properly, these situations will communicate only loss to us, and often this is where the deficit mentality is introduced. Somehow the whisper "You missed something" shows up in our minds, and before long it becomes "You *are* missing something," and thus the sabotaging begins.

The only problem with drawing this conclusion from these painful experiences, even those losses that devastated you, is that in every loss there is always gain. In every so-called failure there is always opportunity, and in everything we survive there is the evidence of sufficiency. I sense your skepticism, so let's explore this.

## Losses Become Lessons

You will never experience a loss without the opportunity to learn a lesson. Losses, if processed properly, are one of the greatest forerunners of success. Failure, if you can escape the looming dark cloud of the sense of inadequacy, can set you up for mastery. We need the vital streams of loss and failure in order to make up our ocean of wisdom and expertise. Often the very thing we believed to be working against us is actually working for us, if we choose to change our perspective. I recently relearned this lesson myself.

**Losses, if processed properly, are one of the greatest forerunners of success.**

I had a ten-year run filled with a multitude of wins. Of course there were challenges along the way, but for the most part success met me at every turn. The congregation I was leading experienced strong and consistent growth, forcing us to add additional services to accommodate the masses and eventually move to a new facility that more than doubled our previous capacity. Things were booming.

61

Doors began to open up to me in the entertainment industry as well. I was invited to work on several projects, including guest-appearing on TV shows, consulting on a network series, and cowriting a made-for-TV film. I landed my first book deal, then my second one, and traveled the country to promote them. My online teachings were going viral, and my impact had reached countries I couldn't even pronounce.

Add to that, I met and married the love of my life, who not only made me the happiest man on earth but whose aspirations and talents complemented mine wonderfully. I was living a dream. I could greatly identify with the title of the hit song from the celebrated producer DJ Khaled, "All I Do Is Win." But I learned later that if all I knew how to do was win, then I was in for an awakening.

Over the next couple of years following this bountiful productivity, I began to experience some losses, and due to my track record of winning, they became very confusing to me. These losses began with a key acquisition I felt was just perfect—a blessing even. I was excited about it and believed it to be an answer to prayer. But after noticing some details that didn't seem to add up, I realized that it was likely a bad deal at best and perhaps even a scheme. I decided to back away from the deal, but not before losing the earnest and due diligence money I put into the deal, not to mention the legal fees I incurred to make the deal go away. This disappointment stung, but it wouldn't be the last time I felt that way.

Shortly thereafter I took the helm of a struggling organization in another state, believing that I could nurse it back to life and make a difference. I packed my family up and moved to the region to be closer and do the work required. It didn't take me too long to realize that the out-of-state organization was in a lot more trouble than I realized and would require so much more time, energy, and effort than I had originally thought.

Not only that, but I had underestimated how taxing the experience would be on my health, my family, and even my marriage. My blood pressure rocketed, my children missed the familiarity of home, and my wife had to deal with the constant plague of problems she witnessed me attempting to resolve as I undertook the daunting task of turning the organization around.

After sizing up the situation and getting real with myself about what it was going to cost me and my family, I switched up my strategy. We returned home to the region where our entities and family thrived, not defeated but determined not to give to the new venture more than I had the capacity to contribute, in order to fulfill my primary responsibilities. I made some key decisions that I hoped would put the organization on the long path to healing and vitality. But the process didn't go as planned, and during that season it felt like a loss to me.

The straw that broke the camel's back, however, was what happened with an entertainment project I had been working on. My partners and I had sold a show to one of the top networks in broadcast television. It was a sitcom based on my life and my family. The network had ordered the pilot and spent a great deal of money to produce it. All of the industry trades were talking about it, and all indications suggested that our show would be picked up by the network for a series order, meaning that we would be able to continuously produce our show for all the world to see. I was ecstatic!

Then the news came. The network had decided not to move forward. I tried hard not to be devastated, but I was. Another loss.

Although I had experienced moments of disappointment previously in life, this time seemed different. My feelings of loss began setting in deep in my subconsciousness. The disappointments were beginning to stack up beneath the surface, and unbeknownst to me, my confidence was fading little by little. It was hard to detect at first, because I was still living in the lifestyle that my former achievements afforded me. But I knew something had changed. I just wasn't the same.

What I used to do easily became a struggle, and I started second-guessing myself and having to fire myself up much more than usual to feel up for the tasks that I once had mastered. I looked at old photos, videos, and news articles of successful moments and wondered, What happened to *that* guy? Where did he go, and how do I get him back? As I began to dig into those questions, I figured it out. I discovered that I had the same problem many people have.

I knew how to win, but didn't know how to lose.

Throughout my processing, I learned a lot about losing, and some of what I learned may surprise you. The biggest lesson I learned is that there is difference between losing and being a loser. And the person who learns this valuable lesson will discover that even in a loss there is something to be won. How we handle losing says more about us than how we handle winning.

Here's another thing that I learned: true winners never truly lose; they learn. Each of the scenarios that disappointed me had lessons within them, and the moment I was able to get past my initial feelings, I was able to learn them. That's what I mean by finding the win in the loss. In loss, not all is lost. There is treasure to be gleaned so you can apply it to your future. Winners look at losses and see opportunities for growth and progress, while others see only failure.

The origin of the word failure reveals a surprising insight. In her book *The Rise*, Sarah Lewis notes that the term failure largely originated in the U.S. during the nineteenth century due to bankruptcy.[10] Originally, bankruptcy referred to what happens when an entity has come to a dead end and cannot go on any longer. Over time, however, the term failure was applied to human lives, which was problematic for obvious reasons—chiefly because we never come to a full end until we die. As long as we are breathing, our lives continue. There is finality in the term failure in its original meaning, but there is never finality for us when we fail, only an opportunity to learn and to start again and to keep going. Usually that new start positions us for bigger and better accomplishments in the future.

Knowing how to lose is about perspective, processing, and not allowing a loss to make you a loser.

## Lack for Nothing

Achieving Balance and discovering the glorious gift of rest is accomplished when we escape the noise we accumulate throughout our life's journey. By virtue of our experiences, our lives are much noisier than we realize. When we don't process our hurts and disappointments, by default they are ill-processed and become noise in our subconsciousness. This cacophony keeps us limited, restricted, and unable to fully show up in the lives we live.

The deficit mentality is noisy, always suggesting to you that you don't have enough or are not enough. Fear chimes in and rehearses to you every possible negative outcome, putting your creativity and imagination in overdrive not toward thriving in your dreams and goals but instead toward merely surviving, trying to escape a boogeyman who Night has convinced you is coming.

And let us not forget disappointment, which may be the noisiest of them all. It makes you question your worth and value. Its noise calls you a loser and tries to convince you that life has it in for you and you'll never get to where you want to go. Night often uses the noise of disappointment to make you want to give up, sometimes on life itself. You'd be surprised how noisy life can get, and the internal chatter it creates is astounding, constantly distracting and dividing our attention, making it impossible to focus on the truth and walk in the light of Balance.

And what is the truth of Balance? Regarding the gift of rest, it can be summed up in one powerful affirmation: I have no lack.

This is what the gift of rest is all about. When this rest shows up, it is marked by the silencing of all the noise of the deficit mentality and brings us into an awareness in which we don't perceive lack. We are full, all things are present, and nothing is missing. When we are in this state of rest, angst and anxiety subside because what is ours is ours already, and it's just a matter of positioning ourselves to receive it. Our spirits calm and we have unlimited patience, because there is no fear of missing out. We don't have to rush things or try to manipulate the process. Everything that exists already will flow into our lives at the perfect time. This is the freedom that the state of rest brings.

In my observation, the most optimistic creature in existence is the bird. I've never seen one stressed or depressed. I know that their feelings may be hard to prove scientifically, but if you observe their behavior, especially when it comes to the provision of food, they seem pretty relaxed. As far as I know, they don't have to clock in to work anywhere, yet they seem to live with an assurance that if they just keep moving, their meal will appear. It may happen in the form of a human's discarded lunch, crumbs that have fallen to the ground, or by virtue of nature's bounty growing in the wild.

Regardless of the how, the need is always met.

I wonder if the reason why a bird sings so much, often in the dawn of a new day, is because it awakens with the awareness "I lack nothing." It's so fitting that they have wings. Their abundance mentality and their wings to soar go hand and hand. We have wings too, but we just don't perceive them much. They are found in Balance and when our rest comes, it allows us to fly above the fray and the noisiness of life so we can abide in the posture of receiving the abundance that is always present.

## The Abundance Mentality

When you are able to declare and believe that you have no lack, it is the evidence that you have entered into the rest that Balance affords. King David wrote in one his most popular songs, Psalm 23, "The LORD is my shepherd; I shall not want." The word translated as "want" in that passage has a very broad range of definition. It means to lack, fail, lessen, decrease, or make lower. "I shall not want" is abundance talk. King David was making a declaration about his life and his future, proclaiming that his life was going to trend upward only and never downward.

King David experienced many highs and lows in his life but came to understand that even his losses had wins in them. He had to hold on to the promise of abundance, even though it wasn't always evident. Even as king, he didn't always have what he expected or have it the way he expected.

I can relate, because one thing I have learned about abundance is that we often don't understand how the abundance assigned to our lives is distributed. We believe abundance suggests that we will have barns filled with supplies, and provisions in our back yards, that we're able to see, touch, and access at any time, causing us to sleep better because we know it's there. But this mindset is not an abundance mentality; it's actually the opposite. If the only way I am willing to believe it is if I see it, that's a deficit mentality. The deficit mentality has no true optimism. Since it expects the worst, it needs evidence to be convinced otherwise.

The abundance mentality is optimistic, joyful, and always full of faith. King David was assured of the abundance in his life and declares on behalf of the rest of us that we will not want, lack, diminish, decrease, lessen, or be made lower. He was acknowledging that even his setbacks would work in his favor. The abundance mentality doesn't see loss as final. It doesn't believe in the notion of a once-in-a-lifetime opportunity. It believes that if something is for you, it is for you, and if what you expected slipped away from you, it's coming back around—bigger and better in the future.

The abundance mentality says that even though you thought you went without, if you survived it, the notion of not enough was just an illusion. If what you had wasn't enough, you wouldn't be here. The concept of enough is evasive, as enough is in the eye of the beholder; however, the abundance mentality shifts the beholder's eyes to see the ever-present provision that the gift of rest reveals.

The abundance mentality delivers us from jealousy as well. Abundance says there's enough space and goodness in this world for your abundance and mine too. This is not a competition. People who are jealous and envious have been duped by Night and are plagued by a deficit mentality. They'll never reach their potential in life until they understand the reality of abundance. The abundance mentality solves so many personal and interpersonal problems in our world.

This is the mentality that we all must have, and the gift of rest will get us there.

# Just Receive

Achieving Balance creates a divine rest that stills the waves of toil, conflict, questioning, and the lack mentality, putting us in the position to receive everything that already exists. Resources for good and our progress are abundant, and just like with the birds, they appear on our path when our souls are rested and ready to receive them. It's just a matter of learning to live in the posture of receiving. We don't toil in desperation for what we have already. We move forward in our tasks confidently, excitedly, because we recognize that we are not laboring to possess; we're laboring because we possess what's ours already. This is the gift of rest.

Before we move on to the next section, I want you to meditate on the following questions.

Who would you be if you had no consciousness of failure or lack?

What would you do—or maybe the better question is, what *wouldn't* you do?

It's my belief that you are closer than you have ever been to the blessings and rewards of Balance. I'm excited to lead you forward to explore the practical side of getting there. Remember, your best never comes from the place of rush; it comes from the place of rest!

## PART 2

# RESTORING
# BALANCE
BALANCE

BALANCE

BALANCE

# CHAPTER 5

# Five Signs of Imbalance

*Life is a balance of holding on and letting go.*
—RUMI

During the process of writing this book, I discovered a powerful truth that I had never considered during previous creative endeavors. I found out that each person has not just one best but two. You may have the same questions I did at first: "How is that possible? Isn't someone's best their best? Either it's a person's best or it isn't, right?"

If your upbringing was similar to mine, as a youth you likely were encouraged to always do your best. Give it all you've got, and no matter what the results bring, as long as you do your best, you can be satisfied. This encouragement to always apply yourself was meaningful and helpful, and I can certainly see the truth in it and the value to those who heed such advice. What my book-writing process taught me, however, is that *best* has levels. Let me explain.

When I wrote the more than twenty-five thousand words toward the initial manuscript of *Balance, approximately halfway to completion mind you,* I had worked extremely hard and had given it all that I had. No slacking or coasting. I wrote consistently and brought my full attention to my wordsmithing. According to that popular adage "Always do your best," I was surely measuring up. It was my best, at least for where I was in that season of my life. What I didn't know, however, was that I had another best waiting for me—a better best I would produce if I could just get to Balance.

## Your Best in Balance

When we are not balanced, we are restricted in our output. We're capped and only able to draw from the resources of our current, lesser state. What you are able to accomplish when you're balanced versus what you can do when you're not is incomparable. We're talking about two different worlds. On planet Balance your abilities and resources are abundant, but not just your resources—you are abundant too. The version of you that emerges from Balance is dimensionally different from the version of you that shows up otherwise. This is why we have two bests. There is our best, and then there's the best we're capable of producing when in Balance.

The balanced version of you knows how to tap into Balance's resources to curate creations and experiences that enhance not only your life but the lives of those around you and the projects you are assigned to complete. When you dwell in Balance, your relationships are enhanced, you parent with patience and insight, you bring creativity and innovation to your work, you experience unmatched fulfillment, and every dimension of life becomes more vivid. Everything you touch improves.

Here's what fascinates me about my book-writing experience. When I think about the two writing experiences, the one when I wasn't balanced and the one when I was, both experiences shared two common elements—the same body and the same tools. Yet the same body and the same tools yielded completely different results. This helped me to understand something.

Sometimes the problem is not you, nor the tools you're using. Sometimes the issue isn't where you work or the business you decided to start. Sometimes the frustration is not the city you live in or the community you're involved with. Sometimes it's not that you have an irredeemable marriage or relationship. Sometimes the real issue—and if I might suggest, the real culprit—is Imbalance.

Now, we were all taught in primary school that when the prefix *im* is placed before any word, it changes or negates the meaning of the word that follows. Therefore, the definition for a place of Imbalance is a state of being that is without Balance. If Imbalance is lacking in Balance, then its deficit suggests that all of the attributes and benefits afforded us when we are balanced are not present. Knowing what you know at this point about Balance, the possibility of being imbalanced should be quite alarming. Let's unpack the opposition a bit more thoroughly.

Balance is the place of ever-present light. It's the space where the sunlight never ceases and darkness is dispelled. There's no Night in Balance, only Day. Because there's no Night, no weeping can be found and the joy of the morning is continuous. Truth is everywhere and lies cannot survive there. Knowledge, wisdom, and revelation consume the atmosphere. Insecurity, doubt, and confusion are nowhere to be found. Balance is a place of peace, ability, and absolute confidence. Nothing is impossible here.

Imbalance, conversely, is ruled by Night. Its darkness leaves you disoriented, distracted, and disengaged from who you really are and what matters most. Because you are constantly trying to regain your equilibrium in Imbalance's spiraling black hole of dullness and exhaustion, you're unable to focus on much more than basic functioning. Your best—the best you're capable of producing in Balance—remains out of reach.

To find Balance is to escape Imbalance, the evidence of Night's onslaught. To pursue Balance is to declare war against Night and its relentless attacks. Imbalance cannot be taken lightly, and although it

> To pursue Balance is to declare war against Night and its relentless attacks.

is a stealth foe, there are signs and symptoms that can reveal its presence in our lives. Over the years, I've developed a fortitude to fight Imbalance, the sinister agent of Night, whenever it is perceived. I've also paid attention to the side effects that make it evident that Balance somehow has slipped away from me. Let's take a look at the symptoms.

## Five Telltale Signs of Imbalance

### Stagnation

If you are like me, you would likely agree that few things in life are more frustrating than feeling stuck. Feeling stuck in your job. Feeling stuck because you can't find a job. Feeling stuck in a relationship or feeling stuck because you're single. Sometimes you can feel stuck in your environment or perhaps in your finances. There are as many ways to feel stuck in life as there are aspects of the human experience. We all feel stuck sometimes, but it's important to recognize that stagnation is one of the chief indicators that Imbalance has moved into our lives like clouds attempting to block the rays of the sun.

Stagnation is a problem largely because it conflicts with healthy functioning. Every living thing in our world has movement. The very planet we live on is continuously moving around the sun. Movement is everywhere. Even when your body is still. Pause right now and pay attention to your breathing. Place your hand on your chest. Feel it rising and falling? That's movement.

We are surrounded by movement because movement is life. Our pulse is movement. It's one of the things we look for as a sign of the living. The pulse has a rhythm that is connected to the rhythm of the heart pumping blood throughout the body. Although we don't think about it much, the pulse and the heartbeat are synched in their rhythm, and when that rhythm can no longer be detected, that life will soon be over.

Movement expresses energy and healthy functioning in the body. Movement in the bowels is a sign of a properly working digestive system. Nerves, muscles, tendons, and joints move together according to the movement of messages from your brain. The human body relies on movement to sustain itself. Exercise is vital to health because it keeps the body moving. When the body stops moving, it begins to weaken both inwardly and outwardly.

Even things that don't appear to be moving have movement somewhere within if they are alive. Take a tree, for instance. I can't think of anything that appears more stuck than a tree, yet even a tree has movement—and I don't mean when the wind blows. Trees have an inner bark and sapwood that serve as pipelines to move food through the trunk and branches, and water up to the leaves. This movement keeps the tree alive, allowing it to remain leafy and to bear fruit.

Stagnation, on the other hand, is unnatural and means that all movement, internal and external, has ceased. If you become stagnant, then Night has seeped in somewhere, somehow, and has thrown you out of Balance. However, if you're in a season of stagnation right now, or you're aware of certain areas that are languishing and becoming stagnant, don't despair.

Don't panic. Resist frustration, breathe deeply, and remember this: Your flow is not gone. Your movement has not ceased. You're just temporarily disconnected from it. You're not past your season, or beyond your sell-by date. You're not a has-been with no future. You haven't missed your window of time. Everything you feel you've lost, even the power to move forward and succeed, is still intact, safely preserved, neatly kept, and waiting for you in the place of Balance.

Balance is our connection to life's consistent rhythm of progress.

It brings us into the current of life that makes the world go around. When the stagnant person gets back to Balance, progress ensues. They go from needing a breakthrough to becoming their breakthrough, because they are aligned with the very essence of daybreak.

When you're balanced, you're incessantly optimistic. Nothing negative can cling to you. You perceive ever-present opportunities all around you. You get up, get going, and go after them. Balance rebukes stagnation. Night is rolled back and dawn's light bursts through. You're no longer a spectator in the stands of stagnation. You're on the field of your life, turning the impossible into possible and making things happen. Darkness has passed and the dawn has come.

## Negative, Destructive Thinking

Another dead giveaway of Imbalance is a decline in the quality of your thought life. You and I can never be any better, in a moment of time, than the thoughts we allow to run through our heads. When those thoughts consistently become negative and destructive, they pull you out of Balance.

A person's life consists of the thoughts they think. Our thoughts are our world. They are a life unto themselves, and when a person is balanced, they exist in a world that elevates their thinking with high-quality, premium thoughts about self, about others, and about the world around them. To the contrary, when a person is not balanced, their thoughts become vulnerable to Night's narratives concerning life, and things can quickly race downhill from there.

I can tell right away that Balance is slipping when my thoughts descend to the lowest possible interpretation of a circumstance. I don't know if this has ever happened to you, but there have been times when I have found myself wasting valuable cognitive energy and time reading into the words and actions of others, assuming some mischief, only to find that my train of thought was completely baseless. If you've been there, you know how confusing and even shameful these situations often leave you. Best case, the thoughts don't spill out of our mouths but remain in our heads, saving us from embarrassment. The mind can be a tricky thing when you're not balanced, but the balanced mind will always work for you, not against you.

To start, the place of Balance is abundant in personal affirmation and self-value. When you know who you are and what you are worth, it makes all the difference in which version of you shows up in life. Without Balance, there's room to question your worth and adequacy. When that hasn't been settled, comparisons and the question, "Am I good enough?" lurk in the fringes of our consciousness, leaving an opening for Night to answer that question with some version of "Absolutely not!"

Insecurity is one of the worst thought processors in the human experience and brings out the lowest level of our thinking. When we aren't intentional about practicing Balance, a discipline we'll discuss in part 3, insecurity and self-consciousness will take over and control the gates of our minds. Once our thoughts have been hijacked, it can be difficult to ransom our mind and regain our strength. But as long as you have breath in your body, it's not too late to return to Balance. And when you're back in Balance, the stronghold of negative thinking will surely come down.

## Lack of Vision

One of the most important functions of Balance is to tell us who we truly are. I never feel more confident, clear, and called than when I am pursuing, practicing, and persisting in Balance. The image of ourselves that Balance reflects back to us communicates who we are, what we've been endowed with, and the significance of that unique contribution to our world.

Our sense of purpose, calling, and significance is clear because it's devoid of the diminishing effects of Night. In this state of undisputed light, we freely receive inspiration and vision for what we can accomplish. In Balance the vision is real, achievable, attainable, and settled. The moment we slip into Imbalance, however, little by little that vision and its urgency dwindles and fades away, as surely as the horizon swallows the sun at dusk. I've been there, and it can be a very perplexing season.

Can you relate to this in your life? Has there ever been a time when you've had trouble accessing the dream you once had or the fortitude to pursue it? Have you ever wondered how you could one day be standing tall on the top of the mountain of your vision, and the next day you could hardly see it for yourself? Has it ever felt as if your dream disappeared in thin air? Are you going through something like that right now? If so, trust me—I understand, and there is a way forward to get back your vision, your future, and your fight. It's in returning to Balance.

Here's something that's important to remember. The vision never moves; we do. What often happens in life is that we get distracted by something, our rhythm gets broken, and we stop doing the things we did that brought us to Balance in the first place. We forget that achieving and remaining in Balance requires intentionality, discipline, and consistency. Balance can't be reached on autopilot. The great news is that you can regain control of your plane and steer it back to Balance at any time. As you become seasoned in Balance, you'll learn to quickly cut through the clouds of confusion, shake off the distractions that drew you out of focus, and return to the mountaintop where the vastness of the vision is clear again.

## Weariness

Whenever you start to feel weary, be on high alert because Imbalance wants to breach your shores. I'm not talking about being tired. That's normal. We get tired every day and usually respond with sleep so that our bodies can recover. Weariness, on the other hand, is a different thing.

I like to define weariness as the subtle, gradual, gravitational pull toward the tarmac of disaster. Let's break that definition down. The first thing you need to know about weariness is that it is subtle. To the undiscerning, it can be hard to detect. Weariness blinds us from our true, depraved condition. It masquerades itself as the more acceptable "tired," creating a dangerous illusion because what you do to remedy tiredness is much different and less involved than what it takes to address weariness.

The next thing you have to understand is that weariness grows gradually. If it isn't addressed, it doesn't get better; it gets worse. We may get better at functioning dysfunctionally with our weariness, but make no mistake about it. Once it sets in, we are on a slippery slope. Weariness has an agenda, and if it continues undetected, it leads you to a sure destination: disaster.

Disaster is weariness's plan A for your life, but it also has a plan B: mediocrity.

When I was writing my first draft of *Balance*, I was weary but didn't detect it. I knew I had been tired for a while and needed a soul vacation, but I falsely presumed that I could afford to put it off. In reality, I couldn't afford to wait, and the evidence was the outcome of what my lesser best produced. This experience taught me something about the connection between tiredness and weariness. Weariness is where we end up when tiredness is not addressed. By the way, weariness isn't just physical. It can be physical, emotional, spiritual, and sometimes all three. Because it is gradual by nature, sometimes it starts in one of the three and then metastasizes and spreads across them all. Additional symptoms and side effects of weariness include diminished creativity, poor judgment, slips in integrity, deterioration of relationships, and burnout.

As you can see, weariness is nothing to play with. There's so much on the line. Night is often behind weariness, stealthily oppressing us and hoping to bring us down for fear of the brightness of our light's full expression. I almost fell victim to Night's assault, but Balance had another plan. One phone call with a message of truth from my literary agent brought the daybreak I needed. I acknowledged my weariness, confessed my lesser best, divorced mediocrity, and pursued the restful state of Balance. Once I was there, Balance renewed my strength, reinvigorated my being with clarity, and caused me to rediscover the highest version of me, which had been lost.

## Jealousy and Envy

I don't believe it would be a reach to admit that we all have experienced a bout or two with jealousy or envy at some point in our lives. Maybe it was the time your friend met and married their dream spouse while you were still lamenting over not discovering a significant other of your own. Or maybe it was about the person in the workplace who seemed to get all of the breaks and recognition, while you remained overlooked and underappreciated.

It's not uncommon to experience feelings of jealousy and envy, but they must not be allowed to linger. As long as you quickly arrest such thoughts and speak the truth to yourself about yourself, you can remain in Balance. From there, you see that the next person's promotion isn't your demotion, their upgrade isn't your downgrade, and momentary jealousy is merely a factor of the human experience and a catalyst for growth. If this issue becomes chronic, however, and you find yourself unhappy and envious most of the time, then you're likely hosting the unwelcome visitor of Imbalance.

Here's a truth about jealousy that is important to realize: jealousy is inherently self-degrading. You can't think well of yourself and be jealous at the same time. It is an anti-you emotion. Think about it. In the moment when you are jealous, you have placed that individual or their situation above you and yours. It's self-depricating and a subtle self-induced inferiority. I once heard someone say, referring to those who were jealous of him, that he had "never met a hater who was doing better" than he was. I agree. Although the doing better part is obviously subjective, at least in the mind of the jealous person, the statement bears some truth.

Envy similarly is fostered by the disbelief that the type of good you are witnessing in another is possible for you. At other times, envy can be about the feeling of entitlement to that which a person is not willing to work for and earn for themselves. In those cases, envy is often a self-preserving deflection from their own sense of shame. Either scenario, or others we could discuss, reveals the dysfunction of jealousy and envy and is evidence of the presence of Night and the agent of Imbalance. The recognition of such things should never shame you; rather they should put you on the fast track toward the land of the midnight sun.

Balance is a place abundantly rich in identity, affirmation, significance, and promise. When a person's life is overflowing in these areas, jealousy and envy become irrelevant and nonexistent. It's impossible to stand in the place of Balance, experience the wholeness that it produces, and envy. You are smitten by the revelation of all that you are, all that you are becoming, and all that the highest version of your life will produce. You're too excited about what Balance is doing in you to be shaken by what is going on in someone else's life. If an event in another person's life is a good thing, it becomes a reflection of the light you are standing in yourself and produces even more light and therefore more joy. Jealousy and envy can exist only in dark places where insecurities caused by Night run wild because of the absence of truth that being balanced makes plain.

## Missing the Mark

Ultimately, these signs and symptoms of Imbalance don't necessarily address the real problem: the lack of Balance. When you lose your way on the journey to Balance, when you allow a crisis of circumstances to impede your progress—or worse, to stop your momentum altogether—then Imbalance is inevitable. If Balance is your destination, then anything that pulls you from your pursuit of it causes you to miss the mark.

Now, we've all missed the mark in our lives; it comes standard issue for every human being. The perfecting process toward Balance, however, creates an ever-increasing awareness of the moments of our mark-missing so that over time what was once a shortcoming becomes a catalyst for change that thrusts us into a greater version of ourselves. To find and restore Balance in your life, you must make sure you're addressing your propensity to miss the mark. Like someone who's lost without a map, GPS, or compass, you will likely not find your way home to Balance without paying attention to your tendency to stray.

This reminds me of a word that draws a great deal of controversy in our world: *sin*. Pause for a moment now and consider. What did you feel when you read that word? What came to mind? Depending on your upbringing, beliefs, or experience, your response will vary. Some people will have an immediate aversion to the term because that word has been weaponized against them or someone they love. To them, sin is a scary and judgmental word, one they'd just as soon eliminate from the human vocabulary. Others won't feel that way at all and will merely associate the word to some evil deed or act of malice.

I discovered that the term means something completely different. To sin means, literally, to miss the mark. The ancient Greek word in the New Testament that gets translated as "sin" means that you were aiming at something and missed your target.[11] This word is not about evil deeds, nor was it meant to shame people or put them down. It's meant to do the exact opposite—lift people up. The awareness of mark-missing causes us to discern and desire the call of Balance summoning us to the highest marks for our lives.

## Balance Rewards

The best we can do in this life—the highest and most worthy pursuit of any person—is to discover, practice, and perfect Balance. Now, I realize this is a strong statement and could come off like a naive generalization that is inconsiderate of an individual's unique passions and pursuit, but it's not. Balance takes into account and makes possible the things that research reveals the average person desires most. Let's take a look at some of that research.

According to a study that surveyed 3,006 Americans, the following three life aspirations ranked the highest.

1. Starting a family or spending time with family
2. Being happy
3. Being debt free (having financial security)[12]

Research also shows that those who are slightly older placed relationships, financial security, and fulfillment at the top of their list as well, but added freedom to travel and pursuing things they find enjoyable. Apparently, the highest aspirations of the majority of people are healthy relationships, happiness, stability, and fulfillment. But what does this have to do with Balance?

Well, everything. You'll recall that soul-awareness is the deepest and most comprehensive form of self-awareness. We also know the science shows that self-aware people make sounder decisions, build stronger relationships, communicate more effectively, tend to be better workers who get more promotions, and are better leaders. Consequently, not only do the vast promises and provisions of Balance have a capacity that far exceeds our highest aspirations, but being balanced endows us with the ability to achieve more than we even knew was possible.

Imbalance, of course, does just the opposite. It locks us into a consistent pattern of missing the mark over and over again. So as you look for signs of Imbalance in your life in order to eradicate their ability to distract you from your heart's true desire of Balance, I must warn you.

Trying to overcome these symptoms of Imbalance with the ability of your lesser self will yield very little to no fruit at all. Imbalance won't cure imbalance. It will simply shift the ground beneath your feet, keeping you unsteady and uncertain about where to find solid ground.

The way to defeat Imbalance in your life is to gather all of your dysfunction and bring it into the environment where the light consumes the dark and all that comes with it. The longer you live in Balance, the more clearly you can identify attempts by Imbalance to pull you away. Can you see what needs addressing in your life right now so you don't miss the mark? Do you know how to get back on track toward true and lasting Balance?

You're already making progress, my friend, so stay on this journey with me. Change has begun. In the next chapter, you will gain a superpower guaranteed to lead you to Balance and help you stay there: the power of no!

# CHAPTER 6

# The Power of No

*Balance is not better time management, but better boundary management.*

—BETSY JACOBSON

The swing suspended over the pool in our rented villa immediately became the main attraction of our stay during a spontaneous trip that Sarah and I took to spend some restful quality time together. Constructed in the form of a large, sturdy, rocking futon, the swing lulled us to sleep under the warm Mexican sun and soothed us with the perfect amount of ocean breezes to cool us off. Being in that swing was heaven, and during our time at the villa, we both gravitated toward this new favorite chill spot. It was everything!

One afternoon while Sarah and I lazily rocked back and forth on the swing, taking in the breathtaking view consisting of gorgeous palm trees framing the vast blue ocean, an epiphany occurred. All that we were taking in—the beautiful surroundings, the noise-free environment, the gift of rest, the innovative ideation, the romantic connection—everything that we were so grateful to be experiencing, was happening because of one little word we had the courage to use before making the decision to get away: no.

You see, in order to make this trip happen, we had to tell some people, some responsibilities, and even some opportunities *no*, and it proved to be the wisest decision we could have made at the time.

Looking back, I soon realized that the power of no is essential in order to reach Balance and, perhaps more important, to stay there.

## No Other Word

The word no has to be one of the most powerful and liberating words in the human language. No other word does what the word no does! Rather than close doors, no often makes sure that the opportunities already opened remain accessible.

Balanced people love the word no. They understand that no paves the road to realizing greatness by creating space in our lives for the things our balance and destinies require most. The power of no has so many practical benefits, and we are going to look at several of them throughout this chapter; however, before we do, I want to put something on the table from the onset.

Embracing the word no has also been known to make things awkward at times and sometimes can even shake things up in your life. Nonetheless, if you are willing to endure the uncomfortable moments of having to disappoint people, sometimes even people you love, or upset someone, some group, or some company when realizing your highest self requires that no, then you will discover a freedom that very few discover. If you can but endure the challenging moments that giving a difficult but unwavering no may cause, your life will reward you generously for your courage. Here's an example.

Within the space of just a couple of months, the unthinkable happened in the world of sports. Naomi Osaka and Simone Biles, two top athletes on their way to competing in their sports' biggest events, made history by saying no to participating in the French Open and the Olympic gymnastics meet. Disappointing not only their fans but also their sport associations, these brave champions decided to choose themselves and their mental well-being over forging ahead. The decision to pull out was undoubtedly difficult for a variety of reasons, including that it often goes against the very mentality that many athletes have espoused: to never quit, to power through struggle, to overcome physical pain and even mental barriers in order to achieve the goal. Quitting is taboo in the world of sports, but these athletes decided not to allow the expectations of others—or those of an entire industry, for that matter—to stand in the way of their no.

Talk about the power of no! These two courageous no-wielders, as well as several others who have recently taken a public stand for themselves, have likely redefined the entire mental health discussion that's been coursing through sports in recent times. These difficult nos they paid a steep price to express may well have not only saved them from a very detrimental mental decline but possibly saved their lives, as well as the lives of countless others who now have the courage to take a stand and not pretend they are okay when they are not.

In a *Time* magazine interview, Naomi Osaka discussed what she learned throughout the ordeal. Her number one lesson may have seemed obvious to many, yet it remains something to keep in mind when making choices: "You cannot please everyone."[13] This epiphany cuts straight to the core of why learning to say no is so vital. If you don't, you will lose yourself—and, God forbid, your life—in an effort to please others.

## Using the No Filter

As I have learned to get comfortable with my own no, I have discovered that my no is a very precise qualifier for people, events, responsibilities, and requests in my life. No filters out the essential from what is merely urgent and clamoring for attention. Learning to make no your default takes practice, but the power of no offers incomparable clarity about how to maintain Balance.

If I am in a relationship with someone who can't respect or handle my no, their response lets me know that this relationship is not worthy of my participation. Far too many relationships in our world work only because people say yes most of the time. Good-hearted and well-meaning people offer their yes to virtually anything for the sake of maintaining the status quo in a relationship, community, or workplace. Trying to avoid conflict, they acquiesce to whatever is presented, not realizing that this behavior actually increases conflict, only turning it within. To withhold a no that is warranted doesn't ensure peace; it more likely will lead to regret and bitterness. This can prove true in even the healthiest of relationships.

I recall a day when, after an emotionally and mentally challenging couple of weeks, I needed some alone time to bring myself back into Balance. At that time, I wasn't as proactive in my Balance-seeking disciplines and therefore came to this realization a little too late. Consequently, I ended up making what felt like a sharp turn in order to course-correct my path to Balance.

Unfortunately, that sharp turn materialized in the form of a last-minute text message to my wife informing her that I was checking into a nearby hotel for some alone time in order to work through some issues I had been facing and to address my weariness. I checked into the hotel, stilled myself, and got into a restful posture. I began to process and pray and almost immediately felt myself gaining clarity and peacefulness, sure signs I was on the path to Balance in a beautiful way. There was just one problem—I didn't receive a text response from my wife acknowledging my spontaneous excursion to Balance.

Hours had passed since I sent the message, so I decided to break away from my stillness and check in with her. I called her on the phone and knew right away from her tone that she was not pleased with the way I left. In an attempt to resolve her frustration and make amends, I swiftly left my getaway, drove home, and traded my attempt to restore Balance for what would become days of working through the complications that the less-than-ideal way I left had caused. In hindsight, and after seeing things from my wife's perspective, I concluded that she was right—the way I left was not considerate. It was true that I needed some time away, but it was inappropriate to communicate my needs via text message, while en route to the hotel. It should have been a face-to-face conversation explaining the urgency of my need and working out whatever she may have needed to feel supported in my absence. The problem wasn't my leaving; it was how I left. After discussing everything with her, I understood clearly and apologized. I had made a mistake and was sorry.

But that wasn't the only mistake I made.

My other error—possibly greater—was ending my alone time altogether in an effort to appease my wife. I had returned home and forgotten all about how desperately I needed my alone time, and after two weeks passed, I found myself back in a depleted place, desperately needing that postponed trip to Balance. When I traced my steps to consider how things had gotten so bad, seemingly out of nowhere, I realized what I had done. I had reneged on my no and was now having to pay for it. What I should have done was clear up the misunderstanding and then go right back to what my soul needed the most. There were many lessons to learn through that situation; however, when it comes to Balance, the greatest lesson for us all is to never surrender our no when Balance is calling.

I'm all for negotiation in relationships, work, and business, including the willingness to compromise and even sacrifice when necessary. There must be limits, however, around what you are willing to sacrifice. I believe that each scenario is different and each individual must look closely at their situation to determine what sacrifice—if any—is warranted to produce mutually equitable outcomes in whatever they are pursuing. Generally, I am willing to sacrifice energy, effort, money, and even time in order to make something work. What I have committed to never sacrifice, though, is my identity—who I am—as well as what I need to achieve Balance, no matter the pressure or promise that awaits me on the other side.

Most of what I am willing to sacrifice can be replenished. I can make more money, and for the most part I can usually redirect my time if I need to in order to make something important work. What I cannot sacrifice is *me*, because I don't have a spare me out in the shed! I don't get to be me again and therefore cannot and will not sacrifice my person for anything.

If you don't take advantage of the word no and add it to your daily vocabulary, you will lose yourself and in the end become bitter with yourself. Yes, it's true that your nos are expensive, but not saying no when necessary could cost you everything. There's nothing worth you not being *you*.

## Ninety Percent No

I've come to believe that we should use no in life more than we use yes. If I had to suggest a percentage of nos you should give to things presented to you, I would put saying no at 90 percent and saying yes at 10 percent. Here's why. Your yes is extremely expensive. There is nothing more costly in your life than your yes.

Think about it. How many times have you said yes, committing to something, only to regret it later? Although saying yes was the easiest thing to do in the moment, because it sidestepped conflict or pleased someone, you paid for it dearly in other ways. I have given yesses reluctantly in the past that in turn forced me to say no to things I really wanted to do and in some cases needed to do. My yes had trapped me. Sometimes my yes was expensive financially, costing me significant sums of money because making myself available to the one thing made me unavailable to another.

We must learn to conserve our yes for the things that matter most, and the only way to do that is to have a hefty amount of nos in our lives. Every person who is serious about sustaining Balance and seeing their life become the masterpiece it was destined to be should aim to employ the 90:10 no-to-yes ratio.

Speaking of masterpieces, think of the power of no in light of the working of great sculptors such as Rodin, Michelangelo, and Donatello. In their own way, they had to harness the power of no to realize their works. They began with material such as marble and brought forth astounding creations by chipping or carving away at the mass of stone to create works celebrated for generations. What's amazing to me is that these great sculptures wouldn't be possible without the mounds of debris from what was removed and discarded—or essentially told no—in the process.

Consider this for a moment. What was brought to life emerged from what the sculptor ultimately said no to in seeking out the yes of the creation they were envisioning. It was the power of their no that produced the priceless masterpieces of their artistry. Without the nos of Michelangelo, we would have no *David* looming larger than life. Without the nos of Rodin, *The Thinker* would have escaped us. Without the nos of Frédéric Auguste Bartholdi, there would be no Statue of Liberty. Likewise, unless you embrace your no and have the courage to defy the expectations of your life's spectators, the world will be robbed of the masterpiece you are becoming.

## No Now, Yes Later

The power of no benefits your balance in another way—by establishing boundaries in your life. Boundaries are critical for a number of reasons. For starters, anything that has no boundaries is a prime target for exploitation. If you do not define the lines for what is acceptable for you and what is not, then other people and various circumstances will consume you until there is nothing left to consume.

If you have listened to any of my online teachings, you have likely heard themes around my belief in doing "life without limits." If that has been your experience of me, then hearing me discuss the need for boundaries may seem a little off-brand. Notwithstanding, establishing your boundaries through the power of no is what enables you to remove the limits from your life that others would impose on you.

So how do we balance the pursuit of being unstifled by limitations with the need to have boundaries in our lives? The best way for me to explain it is this. In the realm of our yes, we can move freely and in unlimited fashion, but we still need boundaries to protect the domain of our yes. The state of Balance is the infinite realm of everything good and divine, yet the path to Balance requires us to be focused, disciplined, and selective and of course to say no to *some* things in order to open ourselves up to the vast world of everything.

## It isn't your no that limits you; it's your yes.

It isn't your no that limits you; it's your yes. Unchecked yesses in our lives bring us quickly to our capacity and often overextend us beyond it. This is how burnout, the ultimate limiter, happens. In such cases we fail to give enough nos in our life and then become sidelined, unable to move forward until we go through an expensive season of reset and renewal.

If we want to truly be limitless, we have to use the power of no to establish boundaries. No now means a better yes later. Using no on a regular basis creates space in your life, which will allow you to accomplish all of the things you are destined to do. Just as limits on a computer conserve valuable space on the hard drive, our nos free up memory and bandwidth, allowing us to do the things we are ordained to do. The next time you are tempted to give away a yes, ask yourself what might this yes prevent you from achieving. Then ask yourself if it's worth it.

When it comes to your yes, I encourage you to become a miser, pondering and giving a yes only after a painstaking process of due diligence and qualification. I know this may sound extreme, but your yes is your life—literally—so spend your yesses wisely. Consider having what I like to call a "yes criteria" in your personal and/or professional vision or mission statement. Decide what things are worth your yes and what aren't. Write them down and update when necessary.

This will make qualifying your yes or deciding to render a healthy no that much easier in order to maintain Balance.

## No-Thing Is Beautiful

Rocking back and forth in that swing in Mexico reinforced this truth about the power of no. As Sarah and I reflected on how many things we had to say no to in order to enjoy our getaway, we started thinking about how important it is to exercise the power of no regularly and consistently in order to maintain our highest priorities.

Life events often put us in situations that apply so much yes pressure on us. Demands are coming at us all the time, even seemingly good things, and often because of a fear of missing out we are tempted to quickly surrender our yes. Life tells us that yes is where all the action is, but over time we begin to realize that our greatest blessings often occur away from the action, in the space that our no has created.

Because we said no to so many things, not only were we more present within our own lives and with each other than we'd been in a long time, but also our lives seemed to settle into their most authentic form. It was like our no allowed us to slow down in order to catch up. Have you ever been there? Catching up in life only after slowing down. Maybe it's turning down what seems like a great invitation—to a party or vacation or concert—because you know you need the time in solitude to catch your spiritual breath.

On my trip with my wife, our no acquired for us clarity of purpose and calling, innovation and creativity, and the strategy to bring our most important assignments to fruition. We began to remember how it was in our simplicity that we had come this far, not in our busyness. It made plain to us how our cycle of success and fulfillment truly functions.

It is in our no-thing that we discover the power for the things we do, which then affords us the accomplishments, financial and otherwise, that reward us with the gift of more no-things that then empower us to accomplish even greater things! Read that last sentence slowly three times, and you'll be able to pick up what I am putting down. If you learn to master no, life will reward you with the success that only your no can bring.

If you take care of no, your no will take care of you.

## Your Loyal Highness

Exercising the power of no may not grow easier until you've learned the rich benefits that no can bring. But even then you will face obstacles, both external and internal. As you grow in self- and soul-awareness, you will learn to identify your weaknesses, the Achilles' heel where your no is vulnerable.

Superman has his kryptonite, and for many people their no-power has its own weakness—the desire to please others. How many times have you said or heard someone in contemplative agony say, "I don't want to disappoint you"? It almost always happens in a moment when an individual is struggling with choosing what is right for themselves over how someone else may feel about their decision. This is often rooted in what I like to call false loyalty. False loyalty is when you, under the guise of being loyal to another, prove to be disloyal to yourself.

Before I go any farther, let me first say that to me, loyalty is one of the highest qualities. Nothing will drive me away from a person, a relationship, a business deal, or anything else like getting a whiff of disloyalty. Loyalty is a character trait that I hold in extremely high regard. I expect a person or a group to be the same way in front of me as they are in my absence. This is integrity, and it makes all the difference in the world when it comes to the environments that I choose to put myself in.

For me, to be loyal is to be honest, consistent, steadfast in support, and forthright at all times. Loyalty does not, however, require self-harm, self-neglect, self-deprecation, or choosing others before you choose you. I can appreciate that in some schools of thought, one may be admonished to think of the affairs of others before one's own self, but I do not subscribe to that way of thinking, nor have I come across any proof that it makes the world a better place.

Even Jesus taught that we are to love our *neighbors* as we love *ourselves*. The admonition clearly points out that not only does loving oneself come first, but it is how well one loves oneself that becomes the benchmark for how one is to love others. If we don't love ourselves well first, we will fall short in loving others with the love each person deserves.

So what does this have to do with loyalty, disappointing others, and the power of no? It's simple. True loyalty has one limit and one limit only. Loyalty has reached its limit when what is required in order to be "loyal" to someone else violates one's commitment to love themselves well. And if there is true loyalty on the other side of that decision, the other party won't accept your loyal gesture once they know it will diminish your care of self. It's in these situations that saying no becomes hard, but in order to master its power, we must learn to become comfortable with disappointing others if that is what it takes to choose ourselves first.

Disappointing someone, especially someone you love and/or respect, will never be easy, but we have to learn to be okay with it. If they are worthy of your concern, they will understand your decision and move past it. If they do not, then maybe it is their loyalty—not yours—that is in question. To be clear, I am not condoning being a flaky, wishy-washy, unreliable person. Others may characterize you this way at times as you grow into accepting and exercising your power of no. Most of us have to overcommit and get a yes hangover before we appreciate the beautiful boundary our no establishes.

Disappointing people is not something we should go around doing as if it's our mission or it's inconsequential. Hurting others by claiming we have to put ourselves first is misusing our superpowers. To the best of our ability, we should stand by our word and fulfill our obligations.

When you find yourself, however, in those rare moments when honoring your commitments and sticking to the plans of others requires harmful neglect of yourself, then you must be up front with your concerns, aim to renegotiate your contribution, and if none of that works, then do not hesitate to offer a loving but firm no. It's never fun but will at times be necessary, and one area these scenarios will help you improve in is being extremely cautious with any yes that you give in the first place.

Because of some of the hard nos I've had to give, I have found myself now with commitment issues. Nowadays, my reliance on the power of no means you almost have to pry a yes out of me. Even when certain items are placed on my calendar, my staff makes sure that there is a little wiggle room in the communication with those I'm scheduled to meet, in case my no emerges. Again, this isn't about being flaky or unreliable; it's about keeping a no readily available at all times in case you have to give yourself an important yes. Too often we reserve all of our nos for ourselves and give our yesses away to others.

This is a recipe for a fruitless and unfulfilled existence. But this will not be your portion in life. You are going to live your life to the full—blessed, balanced, and abundant with nos.

# Thanks, No

There isn't a word that has changed my life quite the way no has. No has been the catalyst for rediscovering myself in moments when busyness and even success caused me to lose my way. No has delivered me from the effects of abuse I didn't even know I was experiencing, until I learned to courageously begin to say no, creating the space for me to see and heal. No has allowed me to rediscover passions and things I once loved and enjoyed that had been buried by the heap of thoughtless yesses I had grown accustomed to giving. No has been a beautiful friend to me, one I will never let slip away. My no has helped me to discover Balance and all that Balance has in store for me. I'm truly thankful and will never let this powerful word fall into disuse.

As we continue moving into Balance, I sincerely hope that you too can wield the power of no to cut through distractions, destructions, and distresses attempting to block your path. We've discussed many tools throughout these pages, but I daresay that the power of no may be your most powerful weapon to both charge toward Balance and defend it once you're there.

Ready to turn the page and take the next step?

Despite the power of no, please don't think twice about answering yes!

# CHAPTER 7

# Balance after the Blow

*Success consists of getting up just one more time
than you fall.*

—OLIVER GOLDSMITH

I love the water. Anything that involves a lake, a river, or an ocean and some type of motorized vessel—I'm all in. I remember once riding with a friend on the back of a jet ski at Castaic Lake, one of the most gorgeous and premier freshwater lakes in all of Southern Calfornia. It was heaven! As a passenger, I loved gliding across the water, free to enjoy the spectacular views and feel the spray on my face—until the driver made a sharp turn into a sizable wave. Immediately I was tossed from the watercraft, flipped a few times, and came to a floating stop on the surface of the lake, all in a matter of a few seconds. I lay motionless for a moment, with no desire to move. Thankfully, I was wearing a life vest, so I allowed myself to just be on the water in stillness. I knew I was safe because of the vest's flotation design, and so I just lay there on my back for several minutes with my eyes closed as the sun warmed my drenched skin.

Something unexpected and potentially harmful had just happened to me, and I needed a second to just be still and assess my condition. Was anything bruised or broken? Was I bleeding or in danger somehow? I needed a minute to process what had just happened to me. The wind was knocked out of me, yet I was still breathing. Although my oxygen intake had been disrupted, I also knew I was still alive. It was now just a matter of acknowledging the fall, assessing the damage, and building a plan to get back on the watercraft—and when the time was right, to ride again.

## When Your World Stops

Falling off a jet ski may seem relatively minor in the spectrum of traumatic events that can happen in life, but symbolically it reflects the unexpected, fearful disorientation we all experience regardless of the trigger. Consider the major disruptions in your life. Have you ever had something pop up out of nowhere and knock you off your feet? You went from everything being normal, perhaps even wonderful, and then out of the blue you get the phone call, the lab results, the accidental text, and it happens—some unforeseen calamity shows up that shakes your world and throws you out of Balance and into a state of despair.

In a matter of moments your heart and mind become destabilized by the trauma of what has occurred, and disorientation sets in. Your peace and sense of security dissolves, leaving you in a haze of uncertainty. The wind is knocked out of you, rendering you breathless. You experience a sense of pain, confusion, and hurt and find it difficult to see the light that once assured a positive outcome.

This may be the most debilitating part of suffering life's blows. What often eludes us in moments like these, more than anything else, is the path back into alignment with our divine place of rest and peace—the place of Balance, where the highest and best versions of ourselves reside. Instead, though, in the blink of an eye, we encounter an overwhelming sense of powerlessness, as if we have been sucked into a black hole of Imbalance, unsure if we will ever be able to find our way out again.

I know this abrupt sensation all too well, having felt it more times than I would desire. Please note, however, that the silver lining in being acquainted with this most undesirable season is that I've found my way back home enough times to realize that no matter how great the setback, there is always the option for a comeback, if you know what it takes to get there. Even in the most devastating of circumstances, there is always a path back to Balance.

That's what I want to discuss in this chapter. I want to show you how to get back to Balance when your world is rocked off its axis. In life we can't escape such blows, but we can weather them. And no matter how indomitable Night's presentation may appear, no matter how brutal the storm and its collateral damage, if you have the right response and plan of action, the light rays of Balance will strengthen your soul once again. Whether you are suffering the death of a loved one, the betrayal of a friend or spouse, a financial devastation, a health emergency, or shocking news concerning a child or loved one, nothing can burn your bridge back to Balance.

To help you find your Balance after a devastating blow, I'd like for us to consider and discuss the most effective decisive actions you can take when you experience a setback. As we unpack them one by one, my prayer is that these actions will become your go-tos for life's blows so you can maintain equilibrium even in the aftermath of life's most unsettling of circumstances.

To be fair, I am not promising a silver bullet that rights all the wrongs and erases all the pain overnight. That is a fantasy. What I am saying, however, is that calamity can be managed, and with the right tools we can emerge again and find our way back to the place where even the darkest Night cannot eclipse the light that never dims. I've learned that if we would only keep walking and do so with a clear strategy, we will find the joy of Balance again.

# Energy-Save Mode

The first thing we all must do when a blow comes our way is go into what I like to call "energy-save mode." This means immediately reducing our work and output responsibility down to the bare minimum, the way appliances and computers do to conserve power. The closer we can get to stopping altogether, the better—and in some seasons, the impact of a blow necessitates that we do come to a full stop.

Our energy is a precious commodity, our limited life source that enables us to fulfill our tasks and responsibilities and allows each of us to meet our needs and accomplish our purpose in the world. It's our power, our capacity for doing what needs doing, and although it sometimes may seem hard to believe, our energy is not unlimited. In the same way that we are allotted only a certain amount of time in each day and years in our lifetimes, we have only so much energy. This means that we have to be good stewards of our energy, strategically spending it on things that matter most, and when a blow comes into our lives, we must reserve and ration our energy the way we would budget our finances if we found ourselves in a recession.

When unexpected trouble shows up, we have indeed entered a recession—of energy. Trouble is expensive, emotionally and often otherwise. In stressful times, we spend far more energy than usual just to respond to the shock, let alone any additional responsibilities we may have already.

To survive life's blows, you have to make a calculated decision to cut back on your output. This can be challenging, because a blow doesn't forewarn us of its arrival, nor does it come at a convenient time when we have very little going on. While that would be considerate and allow us the luxury of a specific defense strategy, that's not the way it works. Trouble shows up whenever trouble shows up and always without our permission. Blows disrupt our emotional and at times even our physical life, and we therefore have to first respond to it by taking noncritical items off our plates so that we will have enough energy to regain our bearings and reclaim our Balance.

Life puts demands on our energy every single day. All of us have to pay our energy taxes if we are going to move things forward in life. I've also observed that many people don't live their life with energy conservation in mind. They go on and on as if they have an unlimited supply of energy, working and moving nonstop until they simply run out of gas. They may sustain their pace by running on empty temporarily, but fumes won't fuel any journey for the long haul.

This mindset of limitless energy is a major problem. If you expend all the way to empty, you leave no room for the unforeseen. If we constantly deplete our tank, not only will we be limited in creativity and innovation, but when the blow comes, it could wipe us out—in the worst of scenarios, permanently. We mustn't put ourselves in this position, and the way we accomplish this is to leave a little bit of energy in the tank at all times. To achieve this reserve, you'll once again have to rely on the power of no.

# Critical and Essential

Going into energy-save mode when a blow knocks you out of Balance comes down to some questions you must ask yourself. They provide clarity about what must be done and what can wait. These questions can help you determine what is critical and essential to your success in the midst of crisis.

## What Are My Priorities Now?

The first thing we must do to conserve energy is reassess our priorities. We have to ask ourselves, "How has the blow shifted the ranking of importance for the things that I am presently doing?" A tragedy has a way of reorganizing our priority list. Concerns once at the bottom of the list shoot to the top, and demands at the top of the list plummet to the middle or bottom.

When your world gets shook, you have to decide what in your life needs attention the most. That deal at work that's been consuming all of your time and energy suddenly falls down on your list and gets replaced by your need to be present for a loved one who's in trouble. It's about getting down to your short list of absolute essentials and putting everything else on the back burner for a more appropriate time.

## What Can Wait?

Many of us, especially high-capacity individuals like myself, fall into the trap of thinking that everything must be done now—all the time. We like to get things accomplished and don't enjoy having things hanging over our head. Although I believe that shunning procrastination is a great quality, I also have come to learn that there are things that can be delayed when life circumstances require it.

Part of finding Balance after a blow is discerning what can be put on hold to buy us back the critical energy needed to survive our wounds. You would be surprised to learn how much of yourself lives inside your commitment to getting your current tasks done. Again, the commitment to execution is noble and honorable and helps make many great people great. If you are to remain great for the long haul, however, there will be moments when you will have to ask the honest question, "What can wait?" Then you must follow through and be willing to postpone a task or project in order to reroute energy to where it is needed the most.

## What Can I Delegate?

Delaying items that can wait is critical, but in your discernment you will discover that some things simply cannot wait. Such pondering may lead you to realize something like this: if a certain action item gets postponed, then it will disrupt the entire ecosystem of the family, business, or organization. If the economics are disrupted, then the fallout could intensify the blow or initiate a sequence of additional blows from which it could be difficult—if not impossible—to recover.

Yes, sometimes things can't wait, but that doesn't mean *you* are the one who has to do them. This is where we activate the powerful tool of delegation. When we are conserving energy to navigate a blow, we must become willing to trust other individuals who have been placed around us to get those key things accomplished. We let go of what we had intended to do ourselves and hand it off to someone we trust to do it for us.

This isn't always easy to do. One reason is because we often believe that no one is going to be able to do the task as well as we would. In all fairness, this may be true, but in a crisis we have to be willing to see the value of gaining energy over completing a task in the precise way that we intended. When both options are weighed on the scale of life, your survival is more important.

It's also quite possible that you'll be pleasantly surprised to see how others will rise to the occasion and utilize skill sets that lay dormant while you were running the show. I've realized this many times when I've had to step away from the helm of my businesses, either because of an unexpected injury or because of the need to tend to a family priority. In those moments it was hard to let go of the wheel, but once I did, I saw my team emerge with talents and skill sets I didn't know they possessed. Overall, I was blown away. In the end, not only did my delegating give me back vital energy, but my team took my organizations to a whole new level, resulting in some adjustments that became permanent.

When you're navigating a blow, I want you to rethink your energy output. I want you to manage it well and begin to take account of how you are spending your energy and what you are doing to replenish it. Even before you endure an unexpected crisis, I want you take heed of your energy output and make sure you don't make a habit of running on low. The way we handle the valuable resource of our finances is the way we should steward the resource of our energy: let's not spend more than we take in, let's budget with intentionality, let's save for a rainy day, and let's adjust our spending in lean seasons.

# Catch Your Breath

When life deals you a blow, you need to catch your breath and assess the damage. After I was thrown from the jet ski, my life jacket created a safe place for me to process the blow. In a similar way, you must find a safe environment to pause and take inventory. This environment can be found among family, close friends, or some other trusted community. This atmosphere is critical, and accepting and even seeking support can be lifesaving. In the same way I put on a life jacket before getting on a jet ski, you should identify relationships that will be safe places for you to land when life sends you tumbling *before* the tumble. Simply knowing you have a plan and resources when and if the unimaginable occurs can provide a sense of security. Think of this awareness as a kind of life preserver thrown to you by Balance *before* you have to sink or swim.

Too often, when we are in shock or have been devastated by a traumatic experience, we attempt to plow forward and just work through it alone. Now, I wholeheartedly believe in asserting tenacity, being a fighter, not quitting, and not allowing life to kick your butt— however, even for the best of us sometimes, if we are honest, it does. Even the victor in a boxing bout doesn't win every round. The skilled fighter, however, after getting pounded on in a round or two, returns to their corner, catches their breath, processes what went wrong, gains insight, and once refreshed, gets back in the ring and renews their pursuit of victory.

In our own lives, we must find our corner of the boxing ring, our environment for reassessment and recuperation, a place of transparency, vulnerability, insight, and inspiration. Rather than relying solely on family, friends, or confidantes, many people find therapy to be a great and safe corner to catch their breath. Sometimes a healthy support group of others who are committed to getting through challenges can be effective. You may have to try something, or a variety of things, to get what you need. How you get there isn't so important;

what's really important is that you find a way catch your breath. No matter what life brings your way, you can survive it and—with the right tools—even thrive in life again.

## Seeing through the Season

Perspective is everything when navigating a blow. Even as you go into energy-conservation mode, you must strive to maintain a healthy mindset in order to regain your equilibrium. Two thoughts must prevail in your mind during these times. Foremost, remember, you will get through this. Make no mistake about it. If any blow you've experienced had exceeded your capacity to persevere, then you wouldn't have made it this far to be reading these words. So let's restore your ability to see the big picture clearly right now. Your life will be filled with sunshine again. You are not an exile from Balance; you're merely displaced temporarily. You will make it home again, where you belong.

Here's the other thought you must keep front and center. This struggle is just for a season. Now, I realize that in many circumstances the word *just* can come off as insensitive or even out of touch. "How can this major setback be *just* anything?" you may be thinking. Trivializing your pain or the severity of your blow is not my intention, so please accept my apology if these words find you in the middle of the darkest time and most painful blow you have ever experienced.

I'm not here to make light of your suffering. I am with you and greatly sympathize with where you may be. I too have experienced dark and unthinkable seasons, from a traumatic near-death experience as a teen to a painful divorce that made me question everything I had come to know. I've endured some blows with the best of them. I've even gone through heart-wrenching challenges with immediate family. My life, although extremely blessed, hasn't been a fairy tale. Nor has it lacked moments when I wondered if survival was even an option.

I know what it's like to be in the fight of your life so deeply that you wonder if things could possibly be any worse. But I've also come to realize now what I couldn't see when I was in the middle of it—that it was temporary. In the scope of my life, it was just a brief season that I simply had to get through.

I realize of course that some blows, like the death of a loved one, leave permanent scars. Such losses cannot be undone, and their outcome is final. What doesn't have to be final, though, is the overwhelming sense of being lost and the consuming grief that accompanies the initial blow. Even when you can't see it or feel it, you must believe that this most painful part is just for a season. It is not my belief that you are ever totally separated from the sense of loss that comes with losing someone you love; however, you do get stronger, discover ways to cope, find inspiration again, and—most important—rediscover Balance.

**The difficult seasons don't last forever and the good ones will undoubtedly come back around if you don't give up.**

I've come to understand that life, although a constant progression of time, is made up of seasons. Some wonderful and some you would never choose. The good news is that the difficult seasons don't last forever and the good ones will undoubtedly come back around if you don't give up. If you ever find yourself crushed by an unexpected blow, I want you to remember that winter doesn't last forever. Summer will resume, and your smile will return.

## Rediscover Your Rhythm

As we learned earlier, the state of Balance has a rhythm of disciplines that keep us in a flow and place of alignment with the highest version of ourselves. This rhythm causes our peace to run over, our productivity to be maximized, and our progress to be undeniable. These disciplines vary from person to person but are part of the routine that, we have discovered, brings out our best. Usually meditation, exercise, reading, connecting with loved ones, and adequate self-care time and experiences are involved.

Just as a car requires an entire system of components strategically aligned and working together to make the engine run, the life of Balance has a rhythm ensuring our greatest output. When a blow strikes, it disrupts that rhythm, our systems begin to fail, and we're forced to downshift and adjust accordingly. After we have assessed the damage and activated energy-save mode, confirmed our priorities, discovered what can wait or be delegated, caught our breath, and embraced that it's just a season, then it's time to reclaim our rhythm.

Please understand that returning to your rhythm does not mean picking up right where you left off just before you suffered the blow. You have to begin slowly and gradually increase the tempo. Remember, blows deplete you in every way possible, so you'll need to work your way back to Balance. Start small—after all, you're in energy-save mode until you get through this transitional season.

Start with activities that don't require much from you and do fewer of them. During some extremely painful seasons, getting out of bed in the morning is a good start to rediscovering your rhythm. Perhaps you do only a portion of what you used to do. Instead of spending an hour in the gym doing a high-intensity workout, you spend ten to fifteen minutes stretching and deep breathing. Perhaps you're not ready to facilitate your own prayers or meditation time and instead choose to play the audio or video of one or several of your favorite inspirational voices.

When we are in a tough season, we must be kind to ourselves and not push ourselves too hard. There is a fine balance between not allowing ourselves to fall into a black hole and not demanding more of ourselves than we have to give in a difficult season. You can't do everything, but you must try to do something when life hurts.

Sometimes rolling out of bed and just taking a long shower works wonders. From there, you follow through on grooming and getting dressed. Often how well you take care of yourself determines how quickly you can pick up the pace and increase your daily tempo.

Try to incorporate doing something you love with something you need. For example, if you love the great outdoors, then do your exercise somewhere outside to connect with nature. Take a brisk walk along the ocean or lake and nourish your soul while tending to your body. Do your stretching or laps at a park or trail where the greenery and fresh air speak a reminder to you that you're still alive and that life still has beauty to offer.

Slowly but surely, work your way back into the rhythm of Balance. It doesn't have to happen all at once. It shouldn't happen all at once. Do it little by little, building slowly and gradually as you grow stronger, until you get there.

Whatever you do, though, don't fall off completely. Doing something is better than doing nothing. I heard someone once say of exercising, "The only bad workout is the one you don't do." We're not talking about being an Olympian when you're recovering from a major blow. Doing what you can is good enough for now. If you start where you are, then you will rediscover your flow from strength to strength until you're hitting on all cylinders.

## Trusting Again

Perhaps the hardest and yet most critical part of regaining Balance after a blow is learning how to trust again. Nothing shakes our sense of security in life quite like an unexpected calamity. Often, without our conscious knowledge, an inner foundational trust assures us we are safe and allows us to move through life optimistically and with the expectation of even brighter days ahead. That trust is reinforced by the good days we experience and the wins we enjoy. Even when events occur that disappoint us, unless the loss is devastating, we generally chalk up our response as befitting life's imperfections and continue with our foundational trust unshaken. Consider me an optimist, but I'm confident that for most people, when we tally it up, our good days outnumber our bad ones.

As long as the scales are tipped by more good experiences than bad ones, we typically do not struggle with trusting life. We more or less expect good things to come our way. When we experience a major blow, however, our faith in goodness often changes very quickly, even for the best of us. When life catches us off guard with calamity, we feel violated, betrayed, forgotten, even hated, and then we begin to lose our confidence that life is a safe place for us. After a blow, if we are not careful, we can easily become jaded, bitter, and can live each day bracing for the next blow instead of believing that better can still be our portion in life.

You've likely heard the phrase "rocked to your core." Which is exactly what blows do—they send tremors throughout the foundation of our trust until our bedrock of belief begins to crumble at the edges. Our core is our foundation, and for someone in Balance, that core is trust. It is the belief that in Balance all is well and all will be well. This consciousness establishes us, settles us, grounds us, and even delights us. Such a high thought pattern transcends the practical realities we face in our natural human experiences.

Yet there is another side of us, an aspect of being alive that's tied to tangible reality and discernible circumstances. It's the version of us that has to navigate the vicissitudes of life physically and, in most cases, practically. This part of us bases its happiness on what is *happening* at any given time. So then there's a part of us that lives in the consciousness of victory over life, and another part of us that is attempting to live out that victory. A perfected version of us living in the same life as a version of us that is being perfected.

One version of us knows we've overcome even as the other strives to overcome. Life's worst blows can't shake the perfected us, but they can cause cracks in our core of trust, the part of us that is still being perfected. Or think about it this way. Have you ever watched a movie for the first time, and as the story unfolds, the principal character overcomes an obstacle and seems to be home free? But then out of nowhere an unexpected calamity comes, and it begins to feel like a different movie. In the end, however, after a series of restorative turns and remedial reconciliations, everything works out well, sometimes ending up even better than before the trouble started.

The version of ourselves being perfected is watching our movie for the first time. We are responding emotionally to every single turn. We haven't seen the end of the movie, and therefore our trust has limits and can be shaken when we encounter the unexpected or face the unknown. Yet the perfected version of ourselves has already seen this movie portraying the story of our lives. It knows the outcome. It realizes that the blow is only a temporary obstacle on the way to our perfection. It knows that the story is still in play and that a happy ending awaits.

## Your Ongoing Epic

Trusting again is about not allowing a loss to define or predict the outcomes that await you. It's about resisting the belief that your worst-case fears will be realized, end of story. It's about embracing the possibility that you can be blessed and broken in the same life as part of your ongoing epic. It's about learning, when walking through devastating seasons, to balance grief with gratitude. It is to say, "Yes, something terrible happened. I don't like it one bit. I hate it, but it's not bigger than me or strong enough to overturn Balance's ultimate plan for me." Trust is deciding that it is better to believe for better days to come than to allow disappointment to rob your hope for the amazing things that life yet still has to offer.

If you are breathing right now, it is likely that you, like me and virtually everyone alive, have experienced a blow or two in life. These curveballs are no fun, but they are part of the game. We can't keep the blows from happening to us, but we don't have to allow them to carry away our expectations with them.

To have positive expectation is a gift in itself. The reward of optimism isn't limited to the positive things that your optimism will attract. The reward of optimism is optimism itself—the lightness, the joy, and the freedom of expected good. It is the light within that not only evicts dark thoughts, hurt feelings, and painful memories but radiates outward and draws the best things in life to it. Don't allow your fear, based on the trauma of yesterday, to keep you from seeing the treasure that awaits you today.

For example, if you were betrayed in a romantic relationship, don't allow that counterfeit experience to make you think the real thing doesn't exist. Remember, just as with fake money, the only reason why the counterfeit is temporarily effective is because the real thing exists. Yes, very bad things happen, and when they do, we all will have to navigate them.

But very good things happen too. And I believe your life's best moments still await you, if you don't lose heart. We are all on our journey, and our path to the perfect place of Balance will be filled with imperfect missteps that provide the teaching platform of trial and error. The beautiful thing, even when it comes to our missteps, is that they too have been divinely choreographed to ensure that we earnest seekers of Balance grow with each step.

Do your future a favor and make the decision to trust again. The best things are drawn to your trust. In Balance, your trust is already there waiting for you. The sun is shining, and Night cannot exist. The skies are clear and light radiates around you and through you. There is nothing broken or missing, aching or lacking. My friend, blows do come, but Balance is there to pick you up, guide you through, restore your rhythm, and renew your strength to trust again.

Balance after the blow is always possible!

# PART 3

# REFINING BALANCE

# CHAPTER 8

# Surrendering to Peace

*If you cannot find peace within yourself, you will never
find it anywhere else.*

—MARVIN GAYE

Welcome to the third and final part of our conversation about Balance—the place where the sun always shines and the atmosphere is abundance, where truth is evident and clarity is commonplace. There's no place like it and no dimension I'd rather live in. Nothing compares with it. It's the one thing that I desire, and my commitment is to seek it all the days of my life.

I'm pretty sure by now you've gotten a taste of it yourself. You've discovered that Balance is more than some nebulous theme in a book that you read about and then nonchalantly walk away saying to yourself, "Oh, that was nice." You've found that it's much more than that. It's real, it's divine, and it's life-changing. That's why you are reading this book now. You could be reading anything—or doing anything, for that matter—but you were drawn to a meeting initiated from a realm beyond the one with which you are most familiar.

You were summoned by the spirit of Balance and the objective is clear—transformation.

# The Absence of Conflict

A major part of this transformation requires surrendering to peace. Now, peace is a very interesting concept to me, primarily because it is not a stand-alone idea as we know it. By most definitions of the word peace, it is achieved by removing its opposite. One definition for peace is "freedom from disturbance." Another one that may seem obvious is "a state or period in which there is no war or a war has ended." And yet another definition for peace calls it a concept of "harmony in the absence of hostility and violence." The result of this process produces one of my favorite terms, *shalom*, which is the Hebrew word in ancient texts that is often translated as "peace" and carries the idea of being whole or complete.

These various definitions reinforce that the state of peace is achieved via the absence of things that war against it. It's almost as if those seeking to define this wonderful reality knew that although it existed, experiencing it wasn't going to be easy or automatic. Peace would have to be achieved through intentionality and triumph but was something so wonderful that it was worth the struggle—or perhaps better, the lack thereof—to lay hold of it. To achieve peace, we must be freed from the manifold combatants in the human experience that keep us from it.

The soul working in partnership with Balance uses the disruption of peace to alert us that a change is needed somewhere. I use the term disruption intentionally to underscore this truth about peace. To not experience peace means that the harmony with Balance that we all were created to live in has been interrupted.

Peace is not something to be gained. It is something to be recovered if it has been disrupted. When peace isn't being experienced, it has been seized or stolen by an intruder. The lack of peace is an alarm to alert us of something gone awry, and our attention is needed to get it back.

Or consider a figure of speech that reflects this truth: "Hold your peace." It is often used to encourage others to remain calm, hopeful, and still in a challenging or threatening situation. Isn't it interesting that it communicates the idea that peace is something we possess already and we must make sure to hold it tightly? The instruction isn't to find peace; it is to not allow peace to slip away.

I'm reminded of the classic story in the Old Testament[14] or if you're into movies, *The Prince of Egypt*. Both are about Moses, the great leader, guiding his people out of slavery and into their promised destiny. It seems to be going well at first. But as they are making progress on their journey, their soon-to-be-nonexistent antagonists begin to gain ground on them, threatening to overtake them. When Moses gets wind of this threat and senses the effect it is beginning to have on those he is leading, like any good coach he provides a strategy that will allow them to endure and overcome their opponents.

Curiously enough, though, Moses doesn't tell his followers to fight harder, to run faster, or to prepare themselves for a devasting blow. Given the tense nature of the circumstances, any of those instructions would seem most logical. But Moses opts for a different plan for his people. He recognizes in that moment a much bigger threat than the mighty army approaching them. There is something greater at stake.

The bigger threat, one that would undoubtedly deliver a self-induced defeat, is the threat that his people will lose their peace, their wholeness, their completeness, their confidence. In a split-second decision, Moses wisely tells his people in that moment to hold their peace—to retain it, surrendering their fears to the power of it—and as they do so, Moses and his people experience the impossible made possible. The threats they face are literally consumed in the wake of their progress through the Red Sea, and that will be the last time they ever see those enemies. Their peace has positioned them to realize their promise.

Great leaders in business understand this power of peace as well. The leaders and companies that do well understand the value of team morale, and studies show that the harmony of the team is a precursor and predictor of future profits. Why? Because our best always emerges from a peaceful place. Whether you are leading a family, a community, a company, or just yourself, always remember this: where there is peace, there will always be protection, progress, and the realization of potential.

# Riding the Wind

As you've likely noticed, unconventional means are often required in order to journey to Balance and access its bounty. Surrendering to peace is one of those access points that can transport you to Balance in a matter of moments. It takes practice to surrender to peace, rather than fighting to overcome imbalanced circumstances, unsettling emotions, or disruptive people around you. But surrendering to peace will refine your residency in your place of Balance.

Often our first response to devastating or painful news is to cover our mouths with our hands and say, "No!" It's as if we were hardwired to resist and reject the things we do not desire. We live in a momentary state of denial—which sometimes lasts even longer—and although I understand our need to process events and emotions, we cannot move forward until we come to the place of acceptance.

The moment we decide, consciously or otherwise, not to accept what we cannot change, we become trapped in a moment in time and lost in a battle we will never win. Resistance is costly, taxing, and in the long run takes far more energy than acceptance. The Nobel Prize–winning American novelist Toni Morrison put it this way: "If you surrender to the wind, you can ride it."[15]

Here's another way to think about it, which has helped me grasp the power of surrendering to peace. I've always been fond of martial arts. As a kid, I learned and practiced Judo, a modern Japanese martial art. Later in life I got into Krav Maga, a military self-defense and fighting system created by the Israeli Defense Forces. I've recently become intrigued by another modern Japanese martial art—Aikido. What fascinates me the most about it is, unlike Krav Maga and other self-defense and martial arts practices, the power of Aikido comes from mastering strategic *nonresistance*.

Describing Aikido in her book *The Rise*, Sarah Lewis writes, "Aikido embodies the idea that when we stop resisting something, we stop giving it power." Aikido relies heavily on the mental disciplines that retrain us not to resist an attacker but to "[absorb] and [transform] the incoming energy."[16] This explains why the size of the attacker doesn't matter when we are using techniques found in Aikido and other similar forms of martial arts. When we do not resist a would-be threat or blow but accept it and become one with it, we can best determine what to do with its energy and how to leverage it so that it works in our favor.

Acceptance is key in this life and goes beyond accepting the affirming, inspiring, comforting, and validating thoughts that align with Balance. There will be times on your journey when you will have to accept certain painful realities in order to achieve peace. Such acceptance is often the only way to access peace. Isn't it interesting that a popular phrase for acceptance is to "make peace"? It makes sense when you think about it, though. As long as you fail to accept something that you don't have the power to change, you are forfeiting a peace that is available to you.

Surrendering to peace requires

> As long as you fail to accept something that you don't have the power to change, you are forfeiting a peace that is available to you.

us to develop the discipline of surrendering to and accepting things we wouldn't have chosen. It's not easy and may even seem counterintuitive at times when we want to use force or take action in order to resolve a situation or remedy a problem. But if we can learn to transform the energy of the unwanted properly, not only will we regain our peace sooner, but we'll emerge even stronger.

# Follow the Peace

How do I know so much about peace? I want to share something with you, and I'd like to challenge you to believe that it's true. And I don't mean true in general for everyone else; I mean true for *you* at all times. Are you ready for it? Here it is. Each day and every moment within the day, a peace is present that we have an opportunity to experience.

In every moment there's a peace waiting to be enjoyed, and when we align with that peace, true progress takes place. Peace is the incubator of our greatness, ensuring that we develop fully and produce completely. When peace is absent, we can't grow to our potential, and we bring forth lesser creations because we cannot bring all of ourselves—our shalom selves—to the birthing process.

I know this because I've made it my daily mission to pursue the peace that is assigned to my life. I've made peace my guide and it never disappoints. Regardless of how chaotic the moment may become, I've discovered that peace always has an escape route if I will follow it. The absence of peace is an inner alert that a change is needed somewhere. As pain is a sign that something is misaligned in the body, the lack of peace is a sign that something is out of alignment with Balance.

Balance is our journey and Balance uses peace, and the absence thereof, to prod us and prompt us to certain actions. Peace is both a path and a destination. It's the greatest confirmation of Balance there is. Peace is not just a feeling of contentment but also an awareness and a sense, and when the sensation of peace moves, so must we. It must be trusted and followed.

I employ the validation of peace in every meeting I am in. Peace lets me know when things are on track and when they aren't. It's a sensing in a very deep place. It is not determined by how things sound, are presented, or look on paper; peace goes well beyond face value. As an agent of Balance, peace is always at work, seeking to guide us down the most accurate path for our lives.

When my peace escapes me, I immediately begin to search for it. Not with my eyes but with all my senses. It's a diligent search that entails questioning, envisioning, and sometimes even trial and error. Here's what this search process looks like in most situations.

- *Questioning.* When did I last feel peace? What was I doing? What was I thinking? What was my vision and sense of purpose? What did I do next? Is that when it left? What does my soul need now? What I am trying to uncover is precisely where my train got derailed from Balance. By asking myself a series of questions, I'm usually able to track down the misstep, which is the first step to getting back on track.

- *Envisioning.* After questioning, envisioning can help to qualify the path to peace. Envisioning is a powerful tool because you can test a direction before making the investment of time and effort in taking it. Envisioning allows you to live in the moment you imagine, to get a preview of whether an activity will restore your peace before you commit to the activity. Considering what your soul needs in order to return to peace may involve envisioning some of your favorite things that center you. Perhaps it's a walk in the park or a drive. It could be a hike or a motorcycle ride, if you're like me. When I find myself trying to regain my peace, I will envision one of those activities and see if I start to feel a shift in the right direction. If I do, I'll proceed and more times than not regain my shalom. You can do it too. When you lose your balance and your peace slips away, try thinking about some activity that tends to settle you. If your peace begins to return as a result of what you uncovered in your questioning and was further confirmed as you moved in that direction mentally, then it is likely safe to take all of yourself in that direction. Envisioning is a valuable tool to regaining your peace.

- *Trial and Error.* There are times when you will draw a blank. Sometimes you may not know what questions to ask to regain your peace, so you will have no answers or promptings to envision. In these moments you must be committed to shifting and moving until peace meets you.

There have been times when my peace has left, and it takes me a few activities until I finally discover what was needed in order to realign with it. I have my usual go-tos, which include breathing, prayer, meditation, revisiting journal entries, Scripture reading, and fresh air, but sometimes Balance requires something new or different in order to keep me on the hunt and will allow peace to evade me until I get it right. Sometimes it feels like a game of hide-and-seek. You'll try one thing and then another, and it will almost be like you hear Balance telling you, "Warm, warmer, warmer, lukewarm—no, cold, colder, okay, now you're freezing."

I sincerely believe that these moments are part of the plan for our development. Being required to engage our souls in order to find peace keeps us sharp, hungry, and far away from the complacency that causes spiritual stagnation. Our senses need to be exercised, sharpened, and freshly tuned as we evolve in Balance, moving us toward the type of spiritual mastery that allows us to be greater gifts to the world we live in and the people we encounter.

The better we are, the better the world around us will be.

## Course Corrections

Sometimes the disruption of peace is meant to make us aware that a significant course correction is needed. No matter how adaptable and progressive we may think we are, all of us have an inclination toward sameness. We are creatures of habit, and sometimes a time-sensitive pivot is needed. Unless our peace is disrupted, we run the risk of being outside of our timing for becoming who we were created to be and producing what we were born to manifest. Sometimes it's easy to mistake the comfort of familiarity with the peace that confirms that we're right where Balance needs us to be. These moments are often followed by the *gift* of discomfort to get us to pursue our next place of Balance.

In my first book, *Purpose Awakening*, I describe this distinction as the difference between good ideas and God ideas. A good idea is something that makes sense on paper, checks all of the boxes, seems logical enough, and appears feasible. A God idea, on the other hand, is the result of a deeper sensing. It may not immediately make sense on paper, seem all that probable, or check all the boxes that would make it a sure thing, but because of an awareness and the deep peace connected to it, you know it's your best choice.[17]

Once that course has been charted by your inner conviction, all of the evidence that proves its validity shows up. It then becomes clear that there was a divine insight behind the sensing that led you to the decision. For this you become exceedingly grateful. Not just because you've been blessed with progress but because your hunger for alignment with Balance was greater than your desire to be safe or to fit into the status quo. It was a reminder of the power of being connected to the voice of Balance, even at the expense of having to quiet your own voice.

You couldn't see it on your own, but it becomes obvious that a Source committed to your purpose, future, and destiny was leading you and inspiring your actions. This is a wonderful phenomenon, one of the gifts of pursuing and being surrendered to the path of Balance. The peace that these moments offer are incomparable moments of breakthrough. There's nothing like knowing that you have tapped into something bigger than yourself, even bigger than this world. Notwithstanding, sometimes even God ideas can get a little tricky. Let me explain.

It is possible for something that was at one time a God idea, discovered as a result of your unadulterated hunger for divine truth, to turn into the lesser *good* idea. You may be wondering how this is even possible. How could something be divine in one moment and common in the next?

Because a God idea is subject to the divine timing associated with it. It remains divine only for a certain window of time, according to what is needed in order to be aligned with Balance. Once that idea has served its purpose, it loses its divinity and deflects down to a matter of personal choice and not divine providence.

## Dancing Lessons

Sometimes we struggle to make critical changes in our lives, in our relationships, and even in our work because such changes seem to go against what we're convinced was a blessing at a certain point in time. We find it difficult to reconcile the thought that something can be a blessing one day and a hindrance to our progress the next. Often we resist this notion because it's too painful or because we fear losing the sense of certainty about being divinely led. Although the peace that once confirmed that the move we were making was right has gone away, we fail to make the necessary adjustments and then suffer for it.

Can you relate? Have you ever outstayed a God thing? You just knew that the job, the investment, perhaps even the relationship was heaven sent in the beginning. There were so many divine confirmations, good omens, and serendipitous moments that assured you that you were right where you were meant to be. You had so much peace, and everything seemed better in your life as a result. There was progress and a sense of purpose connected to the relationship, the business, the association—and then something inside of you shifted.

Perhaps initially you couldn't quite put your finger on it, but something had changed. In retrospect, it may be easier to recognize that your peace about that decision disappeared. The divine peace that somehow communicated to you deep in your soul that you were aligned with the divine version of you and what that version of you was supposed to be engaged in and connected to was no longer there. But instead of searching it out, seeking to apprehend that peace again, you stayed in the relationship, you didn't shift the business or reconsider the work, and you ended up regretting not pivoting sooner. And now you wonder what agony you could have avoided or what opportunity you missed because you didn't respond to the disruption of peace.

These critical moments are even more confusing when the God thing is still functioning. The job is still meeting the needs, the business is still profitable, and you can't pinpoint specifically what the issue is with the relationship. The only thing you have to go by to realize that the season has changed is the absence of your peace.

One of the hardest things for us to discern is how to stay in step with the actions that lead us to Balance. It takes a deep sensitivity and a commitment to awareness to stay aligned. This level of connection and the peace that comes with it is the reward for a certain type of hunger we must maintain. Otherwise we can lose ourselves in the good and not even realize we are lost.

The path to Balance is a dance, and the rhythm is peace.

Trust the peace always. It's there to protect you, to prosper you, and to always guide you home.

## Pilots versus Aviators

Sometimes the path to experiencing the divine peace that confirms our alignment with Balance comes down to how well we navigate the wind in our lives. Like an aviator flying a plane, we need to adjust our altitude to escape the turbulence and discover smoother skies.

And I use the term aviator quite deliberately. I recently read an interesting article in *Plane and Pilot* magazine that discussed the difference between a pilot and an aviator.

When flying with one group of pilots, the airplane feels as if it's moving through molasses on rails: very smoothly with no extraneous motions. We label those pilots "aviators." The other group is doing something that gives us the subliminal feeling that the airplane is continually moving around as it searches for its comfort zone. We simply call those "pilots." The difference is that an aviator *is* the airplane, and they move as one, while the pilot is simply manipulating the proper controls at the appropriate time and sees the airplane as a machine that he forces to do his bidding.

Okay, so labels like "aviator" and "pilot" may seem arbitrary. Hopefully, however, they convey the not-so-subtle difference between someone who sees the airplane as a living, breathing entity rather than as an expensive pile of nuts and bolts formed into an aerodynamic shape. To a pilot who sees the airplane only as a machine and treats it as such, it will forever remain a machine. So the magical bonding that eventually occurs when the man-machine interface fades can never take place. That pilot will never know the delicious feeling of "oneness" with the aircraft, when he can do no wrong because the airplane has become the extension of his own thoughts.[18]

The main difference comes down to how each one experiences the plane they're flying. In the case of the pilot, it seems as if life is just happening to them. They are being tossed around by the wind and trying to respond as best as seems appropriate to them at any given moment. The ride is jerky, rough, inconsistent, and the pilot seems to have little control over the experience. Peace evades the pilot for the most part and is realized only by chance.

The aviator, however, has a different experience altogether. They recognize that the plane is designed to handle the environment for which it was created and understand that the best way to fly is to become one with the plane itself. Aviators yield to conditions they cannot change and embrace challenging conditions as opportunities to discover new flight patterns. Unruffled by circumstances beyond their control, aviators have peace.

Our plane is Balance and yet so much more. Balance is the mode of transportation, the journey as well as the destination. Balance knows where it is going and the best way to get us there. The more we surrender to the aviation of Balance and trust its flight plan, the more we'll be amazed at what we are able to do. This is what it means to *be* balanced. It's to become one with Balance. When we pursue this type of alignment, we become master aviators and experience, more times than not, the peace that always exists just beyond the wind.

## Flying and Sailing

Surrendering to peace has a lot to do with getting our thoughts under control. There is an entire world going on in our head, and we must make sure that we are the ruler of that world. Peace, much like the journey to smooth skies, is about learning how to get above the wind of thoughts that are negative, anxious, fearful, and especially the ones that render us inadequate.

Here's a noteworthy tip for this process. You don't have to fight against the thoughts. Just choose not to accept them. You can't keep the whirlwind of thoughts from coming your way, but you can tilt your plane in such a way that that wind passes right by you. This makes it a much smoother elevation of the plane, requiring far less fuel than it does to contend with the winds you can't control. Getting above these thoughts has more to do with agreeing with Balance's narrative for your life than with opposing the thoughts that do not.

Consider your commitment to Balance through the lens of the word devout. As used in the New Testament, the word devout originated from the ancient Greek word *eulabē* to describe someone of noble and noteworthy character. A deeper dive into the word, however, gives us an insight into the devout person's approach to life, which will help us to get above the thoughts that attempt to disrupt the peace that is assigned to our lives.

You see, the word *eulabē* is composed of two words: *eus*, meaning well or good, and *lambanō*, which means to take, receive, or hold. When you put those two words together, you get this definition of what it means to be devout: to practice taking, receiving, and holding on to only the things that are good and that make you well. This is how you possess your peace.

Remember, peace is achieved by the removal of the things that disrupt it. As you practice the discipline of regulating your thought life, becoming a committed gatekeeper of your mind world who allows only worthy things to enter and remain there, you'll experience peace that flows like a river. Swimming with this current, you will experience the joy of moving smoothly and fluidly in Balance.

So never forget the promise and practice of peace. Not as something we must work hard to gain but rather as that which we already possess, waiting to be enjoyed just as soon as we learn to circumvent the wind. Peace is our guide, and its absence a messenger to us. We don't fight our way to peace; we surrender our way into it. Experiencing peace is a process whereby we learn how to throw overboard anything and everything that keeps our ship from sailing peacefully in the sea of Balance.

## We don't fight our way to peace; we surrender our way into it.

This metaphor reminds me of some facts I discovered about the Pacific Ocean. As the largest and deepest ocean on earth, it spans sixty million miles from California to China, and in some places the water is tens of thousands of feet deep. The ocean was named by an explorer named Ferdinand Magellan in 1520 as he sailed through these mighty waters. Although he undeniably had experienced the turbulence and teeming activity of the ocean, for some reason he chose not to define it that way. He called it Pacific, which is a version of the word pacify or peaceful. He didn't allow the opposing winds, storms, or difficulties he faced to define his jouney. No matter what he weathered, it was only peace that reflected his experience.

May your life be defined by oceanic peace as well—not without turbulent waters but always secured by Balance as you keep on sailing!

CHAPTER 9

# The Balanced Day

*The key is not to prioritize what's on your schedule, but
to schedule your priorities.*

—STEPHEN COVEY

I've learned over time in my quest for Balance that a balanced life
is more achievable when it happens daily. At the core of being balanced spiritually is discipline. Quieting the noise, spending alone
time, fasting, along with other habits we've discussed earlier.

Being balanced also requires consistent disciplines. Once we
become clear on who we are and what the mission of our life is, we put
into practice daily disciplines that put us into the rhythm that ensures
our success as we reach for our goals. It's one thing to have a sense of
identity and mission. It's another to put in the practical work necessary
to ensure that your identity and mission show up in the world.

We all must see ourselves as investors in our identities and in the
missions associated with them. As investors, we have to take inventory
and manage our resources, because they are limited. In this life our
primary resources are time, energy, focus, gifting, and skills. These are
the commodities we use to manifest the contribution that our lives are

designed to bring to the world, and since these resources are limited, they must be measured and distributed appropriately.

Keep in mind that another definition of the word balanced is to be "well measured." Other definitions for the word balanced include "arrange in good proportions, being prudent, pragmatic, judicious, composed, collected, and circumspect." I love these! These definitions remind us that living out Balance is about discipline and intentionality.

Balancing our days is about using our time and energy wisely, not arbitrarily. It's about paying attention to what we've committed to pay attention to, because even our focus is a limited resource. It's about pointing our gifts, talents, and skills toward areas of importance and using them only in places that are aligned with the mission and mandates of our lives.

We have only one life to live, and with each passing day a withdrawal is made on the limited resource of time. My take on "You only live once," or YOLO, differs from the broadly embraced idea which suggests that since you only live once, you should live a carefree, spontaneous life and do whatever comes into your mind. My YOLO, however, is about doing everything in your power to align with Balance and to make the mark on the world that only your unique presence can make. Since you have only one life to live, why not make it count by being insightful, intuitive, intelligent, and intentional.

As we move toward this goal, our lives consist of the questions we are committed to asking ourselves continually. "Who am I?" is the biggest question on that list, followed by, "What do I need to do daily to maintain my identity and fulfill my mission?" These may seem overwhelmingly large and conceptual, but when you make Balance your goal, they become much more feasible.

How? It's all about the breakdown. I've learned that even the greatest task is achievable if you break it down into bite-size chunks. Chinese philosopher Lao-tzu put it this way: "The journey of a thousand miles begins with one step." If you've read any books or taken any courses on achieving goals, you've heard the instruction to break your goals down and make them actionable—many times at the daily level. Great destinies belong to those who are diligent with days. Our daily routine is a microcosm of our lives as a whole. Each day is a gift we've been given to build toward something beautiful, and we must be good stewards of this most precious gift.

## Identity Check

To make the most of your days, you must remember that achieving Balance is not to escape reality but to transform it. It is the discipline of accessing the highest version of yourself there so that you can show up accordingly here. This is what it means to be balanced—to rise spiritually and mentally above the shroud of limiting thoughts and beliefs and become aligned with your truest and highest identity.

Balance allows us to present a different version of ourselves to our circumstances. Instead of the timid version of ourselves making the presentation at work, a confident and assured version takes center stage. We go from being desperate and needy for the attention and validation of others to being so filled with self-love and divine affirmation that we walk into rooms and relationships desiring nothing more than being the gift we are sent to those environments to become. Balance makes us full, complete, lacking nothing, and from this state—and this state alone—can our best lives be fully experienced.

Your identity—who you truly are—is designed to be expressed. You are never fully alive until you express yourself, *fully*. The absence of expression is suppression, and suppression—whether conscious or unconscious—will always produce frustration. You were made to be experienced in authenticity, and when that doesn't happen, a sense of incompleteness creates insecurities and a continuous searching. Many people are frustrated because they are locked into a rhythm of existence that is not authentic to who they truly are. The deepest parts of ourselves know who we are as well as who we are not.

When we aren't expressing who we are in truth, there is a

disharmony that the entire created universe can feel. This is perhaps the ultimate imbalance, the deepest part of a discordant life. Our true identity is the role that each of us has been created to play. Everything in creation is awaiting our discovery of that identity and its revealing. I'm not speaking simply of our arrival into this world at birth. I'm referring to our awakening to who we truly are. The discovery of our divine identities.

Identity is everything. "Who am I?" is the most powerful question a person can ask themselves. Being able to answer that question is divine. This is what makes finding Balance vital. When you find it, you find *you*. Balance is where identity is discovered. Among the many gifts that Balance affords, perhaps the most pertinent is the divine mirror it provides. The ability to see ourselves in a way we never have before.

You've likely heard the question, "Who would you be if you had no fear?" or, "What would you do if you knew you couldn't fail?" These questions compel us to imagine a greater version of ourselves. Balance shows you that version of you, and it does so much more. In addition to envisioning that you, you're able to access that version of you, become one with that you, and step into the identity of that version of yourself. This goes well beyond imagining; this is a becoming.

Every time we align with Balance, a becoming takes place. As we unite with our truest selves in Balance, the line of demarcation between who we are and who we're becoming dissolves some. This phenomenon empowers authentic living, and authentic living is where transformation takes place. The spirit of Balance wants to get you to the real you because the real you has a mission. A mission that will cause everything around you and everything you've been through to make sense and have significance.

When you discover the you that Balance has always known, you receive the ability to live out that version of you practically in everyday life. The more balanced you are, the more balanced your day becomes, and each day is no longer a random exploration but rather an implementation of what Balance has shown you as your identity and mission. Our daily lives should be a practical expression of who we truly are.

I love who I become when I'm balanced. I become the version of me I once only longed to be. Things just seem to go right. Even things that seem to go wrong turn out right. When I'm balanced, I'm sharper, more loving, patient, innovative, and creative. I lead extremely efficiently, my decision making is exceptional, my relationships flourish, and it seems that whatever I do prospers. It's the Balance zone, or as some call it, a "flow." I've learned to call it alignment. It's when my practical life aligns with and reflects my balanced spiritual life, and the world just seems to open up to me as at no other times.

## The Big Three

Alignment defines what daily success looks like for you according to who you are (identity) and what you are called to accomplish (mission). Discerning how to focus your schedule will require meaningful contemplation and planning. We must become gatekeepers of our days. This doesn't mean that you are so rigid that you can't make adjustments when necessary; to have a balanced day, you must leave room for the unplanned. But if you don't have at minimum a general criteria for your day, then randomness will invade and your mission will be minimized.

> **We must become gatekeepers of our days.**

Days have to be managed or they will slip through our hands. We all sometimes wonder where the day went, and this often applies to weeks, months, and even years. It's easy to lose track of time, but if we set forth, in detail, what successful days look like, then we'll be able to look back and marvel at what we were able to produce in our lives with a healthy dose of focus and intentionality. Your daily routine is the critical practical part of being spiritually balanced, and the goal of being spiritually balanced determines what should make up your daily routine. The two feed each other. Being balanced in the practical sense supports being balanced in the spiritual sense, and vice versa. It's all part of one rhythm and flow.

So now I want to help you create your daily routine. This is so important for your life. This daily routine is going to set you up for success, significance, fulfillment, and of course Balance. It has the power to transform ruts into rhythms of productivity and progress. Although I can't create your routine for you, because it is specific to your unique identity and mission, I can, however, provide you with important criteria that I use to determine what happens in my day. Then I'm going to let you into my daily routine and reveal to you the significance of the activities, the importance of the sequence, and how you can integrate and apply them in formulating your own daily routine.

In order for anything to qualify to be a part of my daily routine at the very highest level, it must fall into one of these three categories:

- Things that *sustain territory* I've gained
- Things that *gain territory* I didn't have before
- Things that are of *service to others*

Let's explore each of these categories.

## Sustaining Territory

Sustaining territory is about preservation. I see every good thing that I have accomplished as ground chartered and territory gained. This has to do with progress made in key relationships, business, nonprofit work, and all the major areas of my life. I believe in the power of consistency, and often the next responsibilities assigned to our lives are directly related to how we have managed our past opportunities.

Progress is vital, but we should never be enamored with the idea of progressing into new areas until we are certain that we have savored the spoils of the last mountain we climbed. In my life, I've seen a pattern of promotion that always builds upon the last thing I did well. We should never put success on autopilot and take our victories for granted. Whether it's success in a marriage, in a business partnership, in your company or department, or in the bond you share with your children, success has to be managed intentionally. I make it a habit to regularly check on the priorities in my world to make sure that my successes are still *successful*.

Accomplishing this can be as simple as sending a text message to check in on your spouse or another of your loved ones. It can involve downloading a fitness and diet app to ensure you're on track toward your goals and aren't falling behind. Certain aspects of sustaining territory may require regularly receiving comprehensive reports that allow you to review key performance indicators for your business, your team, or a department you oversee. Different wins require different tools of evaluation, and you must choose which tools works best for the area you are measuring. Most important, make sure you have a way of determining what success looks like for you—with specificity—in these key areas.

## Gaining Territory

Although managing success is obviously important, I don't believe that the highest use of our person is to preserve; it's to produce. Those who only preserve often do so from a deficit mentality. When we subscribe to fear's falsehood that tells us that what we have is all we will ever have, it's easy to fall into a miser mentality. The miser mindset spends so much energy trying to fight off the invisible boogeymen who are coming to steal what's theirs that they're left with no strength to cultivate and produce even more. What we have is not supposed to be hidden and buried for a rainy day. The power in what we have is cultivated by our stewardship, and if worked properly, it will produce, continually becoming even more.

Growth, multiplication, and expansion signal health. The reason it is important for me to have systems and metrics in place to make sure that the things I've already gained are on track is so that I can be free to use the better part of who I am—my creativity and innovation—to envision and implement even greater things. I'm a firm believer that to be alive is a call to thrive. Having breath in our body is the divine sign that life hasn't seen our best work yet. Yes, we'll sustain our progress thus far, yet let us not forget to perceive at the waking of each day that there is much more territory assigned to our lives.

## Serving Others

The third criteria that I consider before giving an activity access to my time, energy, and effort is whether it serves others in some capacity. I live from the belief that the greatest thing we can ever do in life is to serve someone or some mission. It's the most God-like thing we will ever do and stems from the abundance mentality. Each of us is rich in something. We all have the capacity to provide some resource to others without being diminished ourselves. For each one of us, the resources of our abundance will vary. This is how the world was designed to balance itself.

Think about this. What if everyone on the planet embraced the "I'm here to serve" mentality and took inventory of what they had in abundance and searched for those who lacked what they were rich in? So you would have a society of generosity, with people, in a sense, trading with each other and thereby tipping the scales in our world in a most beautiful way.

Of course, that's not the world we live in, and there are some obvious obstacles to overcome, like weeding out those who lack because of laziness. But on our own level and with a desire to be a blessing, we can wisely do our part to be gifts in this world. We can't all provide the same thing, most likely by design, but each one of us can do something.

Some can give of their time and wisdom. Some can provide finances or a certain skill set that will make the difference in a life or a community. Each one of us is empowered to serve in some way, and when we yield to compassion and concern beyond our own lives, we open ourselves up to floodgates of fulfillment and a flow of divine reciprocity that is overwhelming in the most wonderful way.

## Baseline for Balance

I aim to always keep those three qualifiers in front me when I'm planning my time. I admit that I don't always get it right, but having them in place ensures that I do the right thing more times than not. What does this look like on any given day in my life? I'm so glad you asked, because I have a written daily routine that I want to share with you. As you review these items and their significance, I hope they will add value to how you shape your own days and help you not only achieve the things that matter most but also position yourself for a life of continuous Balance. Okay, here's my baseline for a balanced day.

1. *Stretch/meditate/pray.* I start each day by prioritizing myself. It's important that I don't just jump out of bed and start trying to make things happen. I have to get centered first and access the state of Balance. What it takes to get me there may vary with each day or according to what I am dealing with in the season.

   Regardless of those factors, this critical morning discipline will undoubtedly involve stillness, prayer, and some sort of physical alignment. The stillness is my meditation. It allows me to take inventory of where I am and discern what I need to release and what I need to embrace. The stillness allows me to evaluate the current governing thoughts in my head and qualify whether they are worthy or should be replaced. In the stillness I can easily detect any negative, fearful, or anxious thoughts and evict them from my mind. I release the unprofitable thoughts with exhales and inhale liberating truths from Scripture, positive affirmations, and empowering musings.

This is my time to revisit the divine identity that Balance assures me of and take a fresh look at the promises I've received concerning my life. I go through this process to remind myself of who I am before I step into my day. I define myself all over again so that the truest version of Touré can show up and conquer the tasks of the day.

2. *Check in with Sarah.* After I prioritize myself, I make sure to check in with the one I'm doing life with. In my situation this person is my wife, Sarah. Once I have centered myself, I make it a point to connect with her. I'll ask, "How are you? Did you rest well? What's on the calendar for today? Is there anything I can do to make the day easier for you?" It doesn't matter how busy my day is—and believe me, there are no shortages of items that require my attention—I pause to see about her so that there is no question about where my priorities lie. I've made it my mandate to ensure she never questions her value in my life.

I recommend the same for you. After you've found personal alignment, it's important to get aligned with your partner. If you've chosen to become one with another, whether you realize it or not, their life affects yours and vice versa. Communication is key, and I've learned that if you start the day on the right foot, chances are you'll end it the same way. Often it's difficult to stay in step, especially if you have busy lives. Therefore make sure you stay connected with your partner, or you run the risk of slowly drifting apart and missing the satisfying experiences of intimacy and friendship that make a relationship strong and the bond unbreakable. My marriage is not a solo walk but a joint one. So before I step into my day, I take her by the hand, often literally, so that no matter where the day takes us, spiritually and emotionally, we remain connected.

3. *Exercise.* There is another intimate friend that I make sure to give daily attention to—my body. My body is one of the most loyal friends I have, and it's important that I remain loyal to it. Everything that I do in life, I do in and with my body. Even the simplest of tasks is made possible only because of it.

   This is a friend we all must honor. If you take care of your body, your body rewards you by taking care of you. If you tend to its health, it will tend to yours. Taking good care of our body through fitness and diet guarantees that we won't fall short of our potential. I never want to limit what I can achieve because my body can't keep up with the opportunities that my intellect, gifting, and skill set create.

   There are many benefits to exercising. It improves your mental health and mood. It keeps your thinking, learning, and judgment skills sharp as you age. It even can improve your sexual health. (Hallelujah!) Pardon me—I lost my focus there. No matter what physical condition you're in, tending to your body in some capacity each day is vital in order for you to experience a balanced day.

4. *Eat breakfast.* This seems obvious, but you'd be surprised how easy it is to jump into your day without giving your body the nourishment and energy it needs to perform well and concentrate.

5. *Shower and dress.* As a reminder, this is my routine and sequence, and you have to do what works for you. This is after I have prepared myself, spiritually, relationally, and physically, and now I'm ready to present myself to the world. For me, a shower is not just for the obvious goal of hygiene and feeling fresh; it adds an additional spiritual touch to my day. There's something deeply spiritual and very cleansing about flowing water

running over me. It's an opportunity for added peace and to gain some last-minute clarity about the day I am stepping into.

Then I get fully dressed whether I have in-person meetings or phone calls. Getting dressed puts me in action mode. This is all part of my routine to bring my very best self into each day's adventure.

6. *Touch the kids.* Sarah and I have six kids, so I text them and check in nearly every day. They are in varying stages of their lives and, in their minds and on their level, their world is just as busy as ours. Sarah and I never want them to feel overlooked or as if anything in our world is more important than them. So I text them or greet them in some way each day to make them feel seen, affirmed, and loved. I also try to add some unique wisdom or encouragement specific to that day. You'd be surprised how far this discipline will go in your child's life, because young people must navigate so much—including their emotions—on a day-to-day basis.

7. *Conduct an office review.* It's important for me that I have a designated space to work and to do my best to work only there. This way when I go into my office, or wherever I have set up shop, my environment puts me in the mindset to work. Once I take my seat, I size up the day, reviewing my to-do list, sending emails and texts, prioritizing and perfecting my strategy for the day. It's important to define what a win looks like for the day so that by the time I engage in my first meeting, my goals are set and my mission is clear.

8. *Hold morning meetings.* This is self-explanatory; however, I will note that in addition to having an objective before taking any meeting, punctuality is important. I aim to respect the other party's time as well as my own. Starting and ending on time is important so that all I have aimed to accomplish in that day can be realized.

9. *Eat lunch.* Meetings can be cognitively taxing. I always want to

remain sharp and forward thinking, so I make certain to eat a healthy lunch along the way. Lunchtime also provides a break in the middle of the day to recalibrate and tend to anything that may have come up that was unplanned.

10. *Hold afternoon meetings.* Back to work.

11. *Enjoy some Touré time.* This is really important. I try to find an hour or so toward the end of my workday for play. This allows me a daily escape and is a constant reminder that my life isn't all about work or taking care of others. I sprinkle a little me time into each day. This could be a short ride on my motorcycle if the weather is nice, sitting outside on my favorite swing, reading a book, or discovering something interesting online. A brief but meaningful break from it all helps us to keep balanced and is a great setup for winding down.

12. *Have dinner with family.* In our home, dinnertime is near-sacred. Most evenings a text goes out from Sarah to me and all the kids that consists of one word—"Dinner"—and we all know what that means. Basically, to drop whatever we're doing and hot tail it down to the dining room for dinner! We have eight chairs around the table, enough for myself, Sarah, and our six children (when our eldest daughter, Ren, stops by). There's a grace period of about ten minutes, but after that period expires, woe unto anyone who's not seated at the table. Sarah is a phenomenal cook who's always trying new things, and her meals are to die for. Eating is a big part of why we gather, but the family connection is the real prize.

We go around the table, each sharing what the day's highest point and lowest point were. Our phones are put away, focus is given to the one speaking, and affirmation is the response no matter what is said. As Sarah calls it, it's about "laying eyes" on each other, and by doing so, we can quickly tell which one of our children may need more attention in that season. This doesn't happen every single time, but more times than not, this is what our dinner table looks like. It's such a grounding experience.

We are often asked how we balance all that we do. Although there is no golden formula for the type of work/life balance being referred to, there is one bit of advice that I am quick to give. Sometimes balance is about being sensitive to where the greatest need is in a given moment. Then shifting your energy, effort, and focus in that direction until there comes a greater call in another area.

Relationally, balance is often about listening for the squeaking of the wheels and attending to them. Then, when circumstances warrant it, tipping the scale into a new direction when louder squeaking occurs. For our family, dinner provides a natural contextual intersection that becomes an opportunity to listen out for and add oil to any wheel in need.

## Shut Down to Power Up

At the end of a balanced day, I like to take time to assess what was accomplished and anticipate what needs to carry over to the following day. This sustains Balance and preserves my peace before it either runs low or gets totally depleted. Think of it this way. The best way for a computer to shut down isn't for the power to quit because the battery died. It is to close out all of the windows while there is still enough life in the battery to smoothly shut down and to power on again next time, just in case a charger isn't nearby. This improves the overall health and longevity of the device. Shutting down our day should be the same way, and if we do, it will afford our lives the same benefits. There are a few things I aim to do in my shutting-down process.

The first is reflection. How did the day go? Was it successful? Was anything left undone? The beautiful thing about having a routine and strategy in place each day is that you can measure in real time whether it was successful. We all need the ability to assess the efficacy of our day, and having a detailed plan empowers you to do so.

If I missed something or things didn't go fully as planned, I assess what can be learned. If it was the result of my own doing, then I make a note and commit to doing better the next day. If it was outside of my control, I chalk it up to the unavoidable unexpected. And please remember that it is always wise to leave space for the unexpected in your day. All of the planning in the world will never cause life to cease from being unpredictable. Leave yourself a little wiggle room and learn to be adaptable.

The last thought I'll leave you with when it comes to balancing your day is this: never spend to the limit. You should never go to bed empty. If you come home from work with only enough energy to set down your bag, kick off your shoes, and collapse across your bed fully clothed, you spent too much in your day. Leave something in the tank for yourself, or your family if that applies. When you lay your head down, it's appropriate to be tired, but don't make a habit of shutting down your day totally depleted.

Like the computer, you need to be able to close down well. Process your accomplishments and review the tasks for the next day. Read a little, say a prayer, and find a way to get to grateful. Entering the space of gratitude is the best way I've found to retire for the day. If possible, meditate on something you are grateful for that day. Then optimistically look forward to the opportunities of tomorrow. Sure, throughout the day your balance scale may have teetered up and down like a seesaw, but you survived the ride and can surely close it out in Balance.

I've shared with you things that work for me and the principles surrounding my commitment to doing them. I realize that my formula may not work for everyone, but there is a plan worthy of you and worthy of your creating and doing everything in your power to stick to it. You will not always get it right or be able to stay on track each day, but you will do far better than you would if you had no plan in place at all.

If you fail to follow your plan in one day, that's okay. Every day affords us a fresh opportunity to get it right. Always remember, success is not a destination; it's the journey. Successful is the status of those who practice the disciplines of success. You're successful already because you committed to reading this book. There's no doubt in my mind that you're becoming stronger, wiser, and sharper. You're becoming balanced more and more, and balanced days accumulate and become a balanced life!

# CHAPTER 10

# Protecting Balance

*Never stop investing. Never stop improving. Never stop doing something new.*

—BOB PARSONS

Where you are at this point is both a milestone to commemorate and a launchpad for the greatness that is assigned to your life. Balance knows who you truly are—a version of you that is beyond where you may yet see yourself. The spirit of Balance relentlessly pursues what it knows and the subject of its love. In case you're wondering, that would be you. Love drew you to spend this time with me, and I'm glad you're here. I'm glad we're having this conversation, and I'm thankful for the things you are learning and experiencing. Before we conclude our exploration of Balance, though, I want to leave you with a strategy for protecting this most precious reality.

There is a popular saying that goes like this: "Some things are taught and some things are caught." In a spiritual sense this means you will pick up some things pragmatically and intellectually, but others your spirit and soul catch hold of and cling to in a way that transcends your intellect. Sometimes the profundity of divine truth has to bypass the processing of your mind to get straight to the part of you that needs it most. I often say that our spirit regularly experiences divine truths that our mind has to slowly catch up to. That's because our mind often needs the evidence of truth before it can classify something as truth. Our spirits, though, operate with this wonderful thing called faith.

Faith is a supernatural awareness about the validity of something—a knowing about something that is yet to be seen, physically experienced, or scientifically validated. The beautiful thing about this wonderful gift of faith is that it allows you to intimately experience something spiritually without needing to wait for it to be seen.

## Anticipation Activation

This kind of spiritual anticipation reminds me of the way I feel when I'm on my way to a vacation. My excitement and freedom begin the moment I book the trip. As I envision myself sitting in a chaise on the pool deck overlooking the ocean, without even yet being there I can feel the warm sun rays on my skin, the summer breeze blowing against my face, and the frosted glass filled with a piña colada (virgin, of course, for my religious readers) and adorned with a slice of pineapple on the rim. All this starts before I even board the airplane.

This is how faith works, and contrary to what you may have been taught, faith isn't something that you always have to talk yourself into. Sometimes an inherent faith, a capacity we all have, is activated when we hear a truth that resonates within a deep part of ourselves—at the soul level, the place that Balance is always courting. The result is a belief in something we have no scientific evidence for yet but know is true. Such an experience teaches us that although science is wonderful and necessary, it has its limitations and often has to play catch-up.

I wholeheartedly celebrate science and marvel at what we have learned through it. I marvel all the more, however, over what we still do not know. Even on a personal level, it works similarly. The more I learn, the more I realize how much I don't know. Therefore I have concluded that just as my knowledge is inconclusive, so is science, which relies greatly on human research and input. I define it this way: science is the never-ending study of the consistencies of God, complicated by God's prerogative to choose when or when not to be consistent. All of this is to say, even though it is possible you have yet to experience all of the amazing blessings and breakthroughs of Balance we've discussed so far, I'm confident you have now caught the essence of Balance, and the powerful benefits therein will undeniably begin to unfold for you.

Understanding or believing in Balance, though, is one thing. Learning the processes and practical steps that make Balance a reality in your life is another. Practicing the processes and pragmatic disciplines gets you in the game, but staying in the place of Balance requires diligence. Balance isn't something to be left unguarded. It's too valuable to be neglected and will always be under attack. Night will always bring an assault against the version of you who neutralizes its threat to your life and well-being as well as that of the others your light influences.

Every moment we spend out of alignment with Balance is a moment when our truest mission is placed on pause. When I'm not the balanced version of myself, my output is diminished and my positive impact on everything and everyone around me becomes restricted. When I'm not balanced, I become a drifter and life just happens to me instead of me making life happen.

We have to be committed to continuously realizing the version of ourselves that Balance causes to emerge. It takes focus and discipline. To do otherwise is a disservice to our destiny. So now, as we conclude our time together, let's talk about what protecting Balance looks like. It comes down to our dedication to two qualities—maturity and consistency.

# Full and Hungry

There is a very popular Japanese term, mostly utilized as a business philosophy, that expresses what it means to live in and to sustain Balance. The term is *Kaizen*, and it means to "change for the better" or experience "continuous improvement." I like this term applied to Balance because it's important for us to realize that we will always have to stretch to reach it. When it comes to Balance, we never truly *arrive* and are set forever. At least not in this life, anyway. It's a journey of growth and change, trial and error, learning and more learning, but the great news is that if we are truly pursuing it, our growth will always trend upward. We always change for the better when we make Balance our priority. Can you think of any pursuit more worthy of our focus than discovering and actualizing the highest version of ourselves? There's no greater mission.

This doesn't mean that we are to live our lives in discontentment, seeking to achieve something that constantly eludes us. Balance is not life's way of dangling a carrot in front of us eternally. It will always be about loving and accepting ourselves where we are and being confident while on our journey of growth and becoming.

Remember, this isn't about who we are not; it's about becoming who we *are*. I like to call it being both full and hungry. Full in that I am satisfied because I realize I'm on my way to becoming everything I've ever wanted to be and more. Hungry in that I recognize I'm not there yet and growth awaits me. I am both enough and committed to being more at the same time. This too protects Balance.

Maturity comes as we become familiar with the practices it takes to achieve Balance. The more we experience Balance through becoming soul-aware and learning the disciplines that are unique to our individuality, the better we are positioned to grow. Keep in mind that what it takes to come to Balance in one season may be different in the next. What you need to get there at one age or stage may be completely different in another.

In one phase of your life, part of your routine to discover Balance may involve listening to a teaching podcast or attending church. At other times you will discern that what your soul needs is a scenic drive in the car, a long swim, or a vulnerable conversation with a mentor or friend. At other times it may be listening to classical music, taking nature walks, or meditating in a certain area in your home. The pathway to Balance is fluid, and sometimes the evidence of maturity is in your ability to skillfully adapt to whatever is needed to get you there. The pursuit of Balance should never cease, and we must always stretch ourselves in Balance's direction. The stretch itself is maturity, and Balance is preserved by our commitment to constantly reach for it.

## Your Essence of Equilibrium

On my quest to constantly mature in Balance, I've discovered one vital marker that ensures I'm on the right track and growing: consistency. Greatness and advancement in any area in life is validated by it. Whether it's the athletes we admire, music groups we celebrate, authors we enjoy, even the doctor or dentist we choose—what sets them apart in our minds is their consistency. We are aware of them only because they've consistently done something well.

Consistency is the evidence of maturity and the pathway to mastery, in any area. Think about it. Many times, the sole difference between an amateur and a pro comes down to consistency. Do you perform well every now and again, perhaps under a certain set of circumstances? Or have you found a way to master your craft so that you come out on top more times than not, regardless of the circumstances? Consistency is the key to being great, and there is nothing I'd rather be great at more than Balance.

If I am great at becoming balanced, it will empower me to do all things well. Isn't that all that the person seeking Balance wants? To pursue the fulfillment of their responsibilities with excellence, doing what's required of them to the best of their highest ability? Perhaps this is the most basic motive for most people seeking Balance—to figure out how to manage all of life's responsibilities. This is usually because they feel that they are lacking in their performance in certain areas within their purview. They long for the ability to do all things well, and becoming the best version of oneself, as afforded by Balance, facilitates that transformation. Becoming balanced is a one-stop shop that causes us to excel and be effective in the things that matter to us most. The better we get at living in Balance, the better our response to all of the dynamics of our world. Getting better at Balance is proven by our consistency.

So what does maintaining consistency in Balance look like, pragmatically? In the most practical sense, consistency in Balance is about maintaining the rhythm of the essence of equilibrium. Balance has a rhythm and a cadence that we get in step with when we practice the disciplines that align us with its dimension. The maturely balanced individual can quickly identify when they are aligned and when they aren't, largely because they can sense when they are out of the rhythm and flow of Balance.

When they're balanced, they feel a certain way deep within. There's an aligned agreement within themselves with that which is beyond themselves. They have rich peace and a sense of clarity like at no other time. Their thoughts are clear, healthy, and positive. They sense abundance, not scarcity in any way. They don't feel stuck when problems arise; they see obstacles as surmountable opportunities to release wisdom, innovation, and creativity.

Remember, the balanced version of you perceives no lack. Lack doesn't exist in Balance. The posture of someone in Balance is calm, settled, patient, and abundant. It is a state of rest, knowing that everything either is fine already or is surely on its way to being so. If there is an issue, the spirit of Balance says that the solution already exists and is unfolding. When you are balanced, you sense your greatness and you live out your life from the posture of victory. Even when you're in a battle, your peace still prevails. The winner has already been declared. The balanced version of you can't lose. When you're in the Balance zone, its rhythm is evident and you're flying high, even when there is turbulence around you. Because the fact remains that it *will* be challenging, even for those who are seasoned in Balance, to maintain the aviation that keeps us there. It takes focus, intentionality, and sensitivity to soar above life's storms.

# Guarding Your Rhythm

Remaining at the high altitude of Balance is something you will have to regularly protect and defend. Night's gravitational pull toward a lower version of yourself is a force to be reckoned with. It's hard to stay in the air. Your plane will lose altitude from time to time, sometimes even landing, but the key is to not stay there. The smooth skies of Balance are always available and attainable, so even if—or more accurately, when—we fall, we can rise again.

Three areas of influence are usually responsible for breaking the rhythm of Balance in our lives: Night's voice, toxic environments, and the collective thoughts of others. Let's look at each of these and discuss ways to identify them, navigate them, and overcome the effects these debilitating influences have on us.

## The Voice of Night

As we've discussed throughout our journey together, Night, the sworn enemy of Balance, is hell-bent, literally, on causing us to walk in darkness. One of the antonyms for wisdom is "being in the dark." Night's voice speaks counterfeit wisdom and is designed to divert us from the transformative light of Balance.

Night's voice is its greatest weapon against us. Whether an urgent shout or a seductive whisper, the voice of Night is compelling, engaging, and at times difficult to distinguish from truth. Night is the author of confusion, the inducer of discouragement, and the originator of unbelief. Night is crafty and persistent, so the person who will walk in the light of Balance must learn to circumvent Night's presence. Protecting your rhythm of Balance from the voice of Night requires your commitment to the vision you received in the light.

As we discussed in the previous chapter, the reason we regularly ask ourselves who we are and confirm it daily is because Night most frequently attacks our identity. If Night can rob you of your confidence in who you are, what you have, what you've been promised, and where you are going, it will have you in its clutches. Its assault always begins with identity. Who we believe ourselves to be determines how we show up in life as well as which voices we obey. When you have a vision for your life, it protects you from the deceiving voice of Night that comes to break your equilibrium, flow, progress, and growth in doing all things well. A clear vision and your ability to focus on the direction of your life make it easy to detect a counterfeit idea, thought, or direction.

Having a vision makes a world of difference in protecting Balance, but your vision alone won't be enough to keep you above Night's downward pull. In addition to having a vision, you must visit the vision obsessively. Doing this requires that you write your vision down and make it very clear. Put it in a place where you are sure to see it every day. It can't be lost in your stack of documents, files, and journals that you write great notes in but never take the time to review and update. Your vision can't be lost in an email somewhere or buried in an app on your phone. You must write your vision out plainly and put it in a place where you can't miss it. Be extra intentional with this task.

I have my vision on a huge whiteboard in my home office. I go there at least once every day, and every time I do, I am reminded of who I am. The thought of who I am triggers my recognition of not only who I am but what I have, what I have been promised, and where I am going. This is consciousness.

We often make consciousness this deep, mystical concept, yet at the end of the day it is simply *awareness*—being aware of who we are and the higher thoughts and visions we plainly see when we are aligned with Balance. Awareness, however, must also lead to action. When we are blessed to encounter the divine truths about ourselves concerning Balance, we must immediately document them. What did I hear? What did I feel? What did it teach me? What did it all mean? Meditate on those questions and write down all answers. Often as you rehearse the encounters through journaling, you will gain even more clarity.

When you capture these revelations, although the moment of the encounter may have passed, you can revisit what was shown and encounter the moment all over again. This is how you maintain the rhythm of Balance, by accessing the wholeness of those divine moments over and over again through rehearsing what you diligently wrote down and committed to regularly revisit. The anecdote to the confusing, rhythm-breaking voice of Night is maintaining our clarity of vision and identity that Balance generously affords us.

## Toxic Environments

The person who loves Balance and desires to stay in its rhythm will go to great lengths to guard their environment. You've probably heard it said before that we are the products of our environment. For the most part, this is an accurate statement. What we are exposed to has a way of rubbing off on us and shaping us in one way or another, often without our permission or participation. Depending on the environment, this can have a positive or negative effect. If you grew up in a happy, optimistic family, chances are you will follow suit in your own life. If you experienced anger or abuse in your formative environment, without intervention or anyone to protect you, you will likely perpetuate this behavior or find yourself drawn to the same. Environment is so powerful that, without vigilance, it can break the flow of Balance in your life. Let me explain.

The state of Balance is sustained by an environment, an atmosphere of truth, positivity, affirmation, and strength. No fear is present there. It's an atmosphere of belief and possibility. There is a sense of freedom and safety in it. The impact of this environment is transformational to all who experience it. It is precisely what our soul needs to be well, perfectly secure, and strengthened. If that environment changes and we don't respond appropriately, however, we risk becoming subject to a new discordant environment and losing the invaluable gains that Balance affords the soul.

Do you ever wonder why some plants and trees can be found only in some places and not everywhere? It's true, certain life forms can exist and grow only in certain environments. While human beings can survive under very adverse conditions, they rarely thrive apart from certain environmental factors. Shifting back and forth from a balanced environment to one that's sorely imbalanced leaves us dazed and disoriented.

Has there ever been a time in your life when you were full of hope, courage, and joy—I mean, you were on top of the world—only to walk into a certain setting and within moments wonder where it all went? You can't explain how your courage left or what took place that diminished your sense of worth and value, but you know it's gone. Perhaps you went through all of your morning rituals and left the house aligned with Balance, but as soon as you walked into the work environment, you could just feel the atmosphere shift. I know. I've been there before.

## The Collective Thoughts of Others

I can recall a time when I excitedly walked into a meeting with the top leaders of an organization that I had recently agreed to take the helm of. I was there to serve, and I had spent the morning praying, meditating, and preparing to meet my new team and share an inspiring vision that would benefit us all. I was thrilled to both listen and share plans that I just knew the group would rally around, but what I was met with was much different than I expected.

The moment I walked through the doors of the building, I was met by a palpable change in atmosphere. I can best describe it only as a thick, restricting heaviness. It was so intense that it made it harder

158

for me to breathe. This dramatic shift was a first for me, but I would soon enough discover the power of environments, grow from this knowledge, and become a better leader because of it.

That morning I walked down a hall, across a foyer, and through a reception area. Passing a row of offices, I turned and finally arrived at the meeting room where the gathering of department leaders was to be held. The closer I got to the room, the heavier the atmosphere became. Something had shifted, not only in the atmosphere but even in me. No surprise then that the meeting didn't go well, in my estimation. Without going into details, I will say that when I walked into that room, I also walked into a collective consciousness that was not one of Balance. This taught me a huge lesson about environments and the overall impact others have to shape a locale. When it comes to environments, I discovered that the prevailing thoughts will always rule the atmosphere.

What I sensed in the air when I first walked through the doors of the building was an environment that had been fortified by the collective thoughts of the leaders of that organization. Individual thoughts are extremely powerful, but when they proliferate, they become strong enough to shift the atmosphere of not only a room or a building but a region, a city, and even a nation. Collective thoughts can certainly shake individuals, and that's why understanding the power of environment is so vital when it comes to protecting Balance.

## Bring Your Own Air

We have seen the power of collective thoughts play out positively in examples such as the women's empowerment and civil rights movements in the United States. The more recent collective vision to address excessive force and police brutality in America proves the power of positive collective vision. Similarly, empowering women to come forward when they have been sexually harassed or assaulted has brought justice and accountability to perpetrators.

We've surely also seen the negative effects of collective thoughts when they are evil and destructive. When harmful things such as slavery, racism, and sexism become status quo in certain communities, collective thinking infiltrates minds to sew hatred, prejudice, and greed. These complex realities reflect human nature and societal dynamics. Therefore the balanced person, no matter what environments they may experience, will have to learn how to navigate situations in which the collective thoughts of others become toxic. To preserve and protect the crucial state of Balance, in these instances you must take preventative measures.

Let me explain what this means. It took me some time to discover what was going on in the organization I had taken over, but after paying attention to my surroundings and listening carefully to the words and the conversation of the staff, I discovered that it was an environment issue. As I began to craft my plan to resolve it, my first course of action was to ensure that I did not become polluted by the prevailing toxicity. I had to find a way to protect myself so that I didn't become contaminated in the environment and lose my ability to bring my best to the opportunity and effect change.

I had to do what I have come to describe as "bringing my own air." You won't always get to choose what environment you are born in, placed in, or called to live in or work in. What you *can* choose is whether you are going to affect the environment or allow the environment to affect you. The latter will happen by default if you have no strategy to produce a different outcome. The former requires intentionality, focus, and skills but can undoubtedly be achieved.

Never forget that you are a force, all by yourself. There's enough power in you—the balanced version of you—to shift nearly any environment for the better. Your Balance is the ultimate air freshener! Let us not forget some of the great heroes of old whose voices and spirits changed the world during the times they lived in. It may take time, and in some cases change will be fully achieved long after you are gone, but you have the ability to set change in motion, trusting that one day it will be realized.

After my observations, the first thing I did was shore up my personal environment, or inner "air space," which has to do with my thoughts, my posture of heart, and my belief in the positive out- comes that were possible. Every morning, I remained steadfast in my daily disciplines to achieve

**You have the ability to set change in motion, trusting that one day it will be realized.**

Balance. I spent time each morning looking at myself in the mirror of Balance. I allowed truth to affirm me in who I was, in the unique ability I possessed, and in my belief in the power to effect change that my life was endowed with.

It also was important to me that my heart was positioned in a spirit of love and humility, not disdain and self-righteousness. The staff needed to know that I was for them and had the organization's best interests at heart, so I could garner the type of trust that would lessen the resistance to atmospheric change. Being solid in these perspectives enabled me to walk through those doors each day determined to be the embodiment of the environment I was intending to create.

I must admit, it was more than a notion to not be swayed by the prevailing environment, and some days I did better than others. But when everything was tallied, I discovered that the environment within me was greater than the environment around me. Slowly but surely, as I leveraged my platform as CEO and, more important, my voice as CSO (Chief Serving Officer), I watched the environment shift and become what it always had the potential to be.

I want to be fully transparent with you. This season of changing the organization's environment was very possibly the most difficult season of my life. What it required put strains on everything that was important to me, including my health—which reminds me to insert this word of caution. Make sure that the environment you are choosing to change is worthy of you and one that you're sure you've been divinely called to. We are not called to change every environment, and staying in one's lane is a critical virtue. However, if you are called to shift an environment, whether it's a family, workplace, community, city, or nation, the balanced you is well equipped to accomplish it. Challenging and costly as such a shift may prove to be, the benefits and rewards of transformation far outweigh the costs.

## Power to Pivot with People

People can be significant contributors not only to your personal alignment with Balance but also to the balanced atmosphere you are attempting to create in an environment you have been called to change. People matter. The people we have around us will either make us or break us. They will either facilitate and strengthen our vision or hinder us by becoming weights that slow us down or by pulling our team in the opposite direction. The person who will remain balanced must make calculated and intentional decisions concerning people and relationships.

After I protected my Balance by bringing my own air into the new environment, I found it prudent to intently observe the people in it. After all, if I was going to change the air of the organization, I would need to address the individuals whose collective thoughts created that air. A huge part in shifting an environment is to shift the people in the environment, *if* you are able to shift them. Let me be clear: that's a huge if. Allow me to explain what I mean.

I can recall a conversation I once had with my manager, Dusty, when I worked as a junior sales rep for a technology company in my early twenties. He was sharing with me his belief that people usually cannot or will not ever change. Dusty was a relatively successful person in my eyes at the time, and his words stuck with me for quite a while. Over time I've come to have a slightly different view of people and their ability and propensity to change, but for a season his words shaped my expectations of others.

I found myself in the earlier days of my leadership being quick to remove people who were constantly getting it wrong. I believed it was a great leadership strength to have what I used to boastfully call the "gift of goodbye." Although I do believe that being able to say goodbye to the wrong relationships or situations when appropriate requires fortitude and skill, I also know we can miss valuable opportunities when we simply throw people away before doing everything possible to understand them, and attempt to influence within them the change we need to see. It's not always possible to lead them on a mutually beneficial path, and to Dusty's point, some people are stuck or simply do not wish to change. The right people, however, with the proper guidance, will.

Sometimes you will be the difference maker in someone's life, and as you grow in your love for people, your belief in people, and your development as an informed, skilled, and intentional leader, you will be shocked not only by the shift in the person but by the impact they can have on your business and its atmosphere. Some of my greatest team members and employees benefited from my investment in their potential early on. This is true even in some of my friendships. The challenge is in discerning who stays and who must go in order to preserve your Balance and fulfill your mission.

I often share this valuable principle in The Called, my leadership training workshops.[19] *Some people will have to grow into your vision; others will have to go for the sake of your vision.* Maturity comes down to knowing the difference. I've discovered that experience will be your best teacher concerning such discernment, and in time you'll have a knack for it.

When it came to clearing up the air pollution from the team I inherited, there were some people that my fresh air was able to reach and revive, and others who were best suited to work elsewhere. One important aspect of bringing new life involved paying close attention to the words used by the various team members I was evaluating. People will teach you everything you need to know about them, if you simply pay attention over a period of time. Sure, there are those whose words don't line up with their actions, those who say one thing and do another, but for the most part if you listen to a person long enough, they will tell you who they truly are.

There is a teaching in the New Testament that reads, "Out of the abundance of the heart the mouth speaks."[20] This ancient truth is spot on today. What's inside the heart will come out of the mouth sooner or later, and this will afford you clues about who that person is and how they may affect your Balance. After observing the words and actions of my group for several weeks, it was obvious who was able to grow into the vision and who should go for the sake of the vision.

Eventually I had to make some tough decisions in both directions, but the positive shift in the environment was worth it. I retained some and released others, but at the end of day, the health of the organization improved. I had maintained my Balance and eventually changed the atmosphere and entire culture of the organization. Not only did I not lose myself, but I brought transformation to a team that had remarkable potential; they just needed to breathe the right air.

I'm convinced that the Balance you work diligently to achieve and sustain, with the proper disciplines, can undeniably be preserved. Yes, you will have to work hard to guard and protect it because of its extreme value, but Balance is more than worth your protective measures. Keep it safe and never take it for granted. Balance is everything, and every good thing that is assigned to show up in your life, as well as what is supposed to happen through your life, hangs in the balance—of your Balance.

My friend, it's been a joy to journey with you on your path to Balance. We've discussed so many things throughout these pages— thoughts, ideas, suggestions, and disciplines that you can revisit over and over again. I'll be revisiting them too, as we are all on our path to the perfect place of Balance. This journey is a lifelong process, and transformation doesn't happen overnight. There will be missteps, but if you allow them to, they will provide the teaching platform of trial and error. The beautiful thing about our missteps is that they too have been divinely choreographed to ensure that the earnest seeker of Balance grows with each step.

It has been my honor to share my blueprint for Balance with you. It is my prayer—as it is with everything I write, say, produce, or post—that our time together has left you better than when I found you.

Much love and many blessings!

# Afterword

When I write books, I write them with the broadest audiences in mind. I don't write them to one group; I write them to all of humanity. Although we are diverse and wonderfully distinct from one another, we all have certain similarities and commonalities. We all want to be loved, honored, cherished, and respected. We have questions, curiosities, beliefs, and doubts. We are all journeying, learning, growing, and prayerfully getting better and better along the way.

I'm a believer—a Christian, if you fancy specificity. And I say Christian not as one who espouses religious dogma or closed-minded exclusivity, as some perhaps may express their faith, but rather as one who is thoroughly convinced concerning the person, purpose, and principles of Jesus. It's through this unique insight into and relationship with Jesus that I have experienced more treasures in this life than I can count. But one of the greatest treasures I've received, the one that has brought us together and into this very special moment on our journey, is the revelation of Balance.

From this perspective, I find it honest and appropriate to invite you, if you desire, to dig deeper into my understanding of Balance and to take a peek into the foundational insights that brought me to what I believe are the liberating and inspiring truths you discovered throughout this book. I sincerely believe they will aid you too on your journey in life. If you choose not to go farther into this personal discourse with me, I believe that you have been greatly equipped by the universal principles that we have covered so far. However, if you are compelled to explore more deeply the spiritual underpinnings that motivated this work, I invite you to walk a little farther with me. If you're still reading, and at this point it's obvious that you are, I have provided two options to assist you, and of course you're more than welcome to utilize them both.

The first, albeit a less comprehensive and interactive option, is to finish reading this chapter to get a general idea of how my faith shaped the lens through which I perceive Balance. The other option, useful also for additional support, is to visit *www.TheBalanceBook.com* to ask questions, discover more resources, and watch a series of videos from me that I believe will further enrich you concerning your path to Balance. Since you are obviously still reading, I can safely deduce that you have chosen at minimum the option to read on. I'm glad you did. Now, let's look at Balance through the lens of the faith that has transformed my life in every meaningful way.

Foremost, I've come to discover that Jesus is the ultimate door to the realm of Balance. Balance, decoded, references the uncontested and uncontaminated dimension of our almighty Creator. We would be well suited to call this place Heaven, yet I'm not referring to a place that may solely exist as a resting place for all good people when they die. The Heaven that I'm describing offers so much more, and we don't have to wait until the afterlife to experience it. I'm talking about the Heaven that starts on earth after we, through the endowment of Jesus activated by our belief in him, overcome everything in our internal, spiritual, and emotional universe and align our spirits, souls, and minds with our divine identity in heaven.

I know that was a mouthful, so let me unpack it a little. You heard me right. There is a timeless, flawless, divinely created image of you in the heavenly realm—the land this book describes as Balance. This version of you lives in constant light, with no fear of or even any consciousness of darkness or Night. This identity of you was formed in pure Love and is sustained in Love's darkness-free environment and therefore is immune to the brokenness and blindness that Night and fear unleashes on everyone who has yet to discover the place where the sun—or better, the *Son*—never stops shining.

Jesus, Son of the God of heaven, secured our access to our forever spiritual home by stepping out of the infinite realm where Balance, the manifest presence of God, is experienced without hindrance, and into the finite realm in order to free us to reclaim our place, our true identity, and our victory in this life and the one to come. He accomplishes this through first taking on and literally becoming the mark-missing dysfunction (*sin*) we inherited when we entered into the flawed, finite, and temporal dimension of time and space. His very public death on the cross was for all intents and purposes less about his own death and more about what he was putting to death for humanity. He was putting to death sin so that we would be free from every hindrance that caused and causes us to miss the mark from the very moment we were born into this world.

When we are born into this environment, we become a product of it, and we remain so until we meet Jesus and he reveals to us that this broken environment is not our home. Although this may have been our place of birth, it isn't our place of origin. We have a divine citizenship in heaven, the land of eternal Balance, and we will never truly know who we are, nor the divine nature that we possess, unless we make it a point to connect with our heavenly roots.

Jesus further accomplishes his mission of bringing us into the victory and abundance of our divine commonwealth by clearing the path for the Holy Spirit (the spirit of Balance), the divine agent of transformation, to come into our lives. When we say yes to Jesus, the Holy Spirit receives permission to come into our lives and get right to work.

The Holy Spirit helps us in several ways. He leads us into the path of truth. He affirms our highest identity and begins to work on any lie that Night (aka the enemy, the devil, Satan, Lucifer, or any other name you want to attribute to the ultimate source of deception, thievery, death, and destruction) has caused us to believe about ourselves, life, God, and the world around us. The Holy Spirit starts us on our journey to becoming whole and discovering the realm of Balance. This journey involves a continuous spiritual growth unfolding beautifully over the span of our lives. We begin to walk out of the limitations, restrictions, and shortcomings of our humanity and into the joys and freedoms of our divinity through our continuous visitations to the heavenly realm that we've learned to call Balance.

The more we visit, the more we change. The more we peer into the mirror of our true selves, the more we are able to reflect that image and express our highest self in our everyday lives. Our best self is the version of ourselves that is yielded to the Holy Spirit and spends time in the pure and perfect presence of God, who endows us with the wholeness, peace, and precision each day to do all things well. Living in Balance doesn't happen through random and sporadic trips but rather through a commitment to a disciplined life and a relationship with Jesus, the threshold that leads to everything we desire to be and then some.

I wonder if in this very moment you feel touched inwardly in a unique and unusual way. You've enjoyed the universal wisdom and the insightful revelations you read throughout the pages of this book yet found yourself left without the final spark that would activate the truths of this book in your life. I am wondering if the revelation of Jesus and his connection to the Balance you have longed for is causing this concept to go much farther than crystallization and into a sense of calling. If that is the case for you, let's set forth for your consideration that this call is coming from the God of Balance, the Father of all creation, the Prince of Peace, who desires relationship with you. The one who takes pleasure in the prosperity of his children and desires that they have life that is abundant in everything good.

If you do sense this call upon your heart, you need only to trust that it is a good thing. Allow the peace of the invitation to overwhelm your heart, opening it to blossom as a flower does when the sun's rays beckon its beauty. You, like the flower, are budding and primed to blossom until full bloom, when your inherent beauty becomes evident for everything around you to experience and be transformed by.

If this is where you are, simply recite the following prayer with me and walk through the door that will lead you to more than a life of Balance; it will lead you into an eternal life that triumphs over everything negative and evil, including death itself. There's a place in God's perfect domain with your name on it. Now is your time. If I am describing you, say this prayer with me:

"Dear God, I feel your presence upon me right now. I feel your love knocking on the door of my heart. I am choosing to open it. Lord, I trust you and invite you into my heart with thanksgiving for all that you have done for me and all you have in store for me. Your plans for me are good and not evil. Plans to prosper me and not to harm me. To give me a future and a hope. Lord, I thank you for Jesus. Thank you for making him, who had no sin, to become all of mine. He became all of my weakness and shortcomings. My mistakes and wrongdoings. My brokenness and my flaws. He became everything that causes me to miss the mark and nailed it to his body on the cross of his death. When he died, so did those things that held me back. When he rose from death free and victorious, because I am now in him I rose too. Through my faith in Jesus, I now have a seat of victory in Jesus, far above the limited dimension of my earthly existence. I have a place and an identity in the highest of heavens with Christ. I am forgetting what is behind me and reaching forward and upward toward those things that are now before me. I'm reaching toward the high mark of my life and becoming everything God created me to be. I thank you that with Jesus comes my salvation, my balance, and every good thing that God has prepared for me. I thank you for this great gift. In Jesus' name I pray. Amen."

Beloved, if you took that step with me, allow me to be the first to say welcome to the kingdom of God! The step that you have just taken is one that you will never forget nor regret. This moment transcends religion and rules, things that tend to divide humanity. This is so much bigger than that. This moment is about a reunion between your soul and its Maker. This is the beginning of a wonderful journey that will prove fruitful in ways you wouldn't imagine were possible. I'm so excited for you.

I want us to stay connected. I want to learn of your progress and also make my staff and resources available to you, as I believe you're going to find so many things in our library of content and curriculum that will aid you, answer any questions you may have, and empower you to walk out the most blessed and balanced life possible.

Thank you so much for the privilege of journeying with you. I love you dearly and will be holding you closely in my prayers as you journey forward with God and on to Balance. Take good care, and I'm looking forward to seeing you online.

# Acknowledgments

Writing a book never ceases to be equally the most rewarding thing I ever get to do and the most challenging thing imaginable. It requires that many things, both internally and externally, align properly to create the space that allows my greatest ideas to come forth. None of this happens without individuals and teams that grant me the grace to do my best work, and ensure that it reaches as many people as possible. I'd like to recognize my village, without whose collective contribution, Balance would not be possible.

I'd like to thank my literary agent, Jan Miller—aka "The G.O.A.T."—and the entire team at Dupree Miller and Associates, who encouraged me in my vision for Balance, challenged me when it fell short of exceptional, and corralled the vital professional partnerships required to give this vision the major publication it deserved. I can't thank you enough!

I'd like to thank my publisher, Zondervan, for their first-class and streamlined process of bringing this project to market. It was a pleasure to partner once again with such a stellar group of professionals. Thank you for demonstrating the reason Zondervan is recognized as a leading and world-class publisher.

I'd like to thank Dudley Delffs for the added texture and framing that he brought to Balance. Dudley, I entrusted you with a great book. You added your touch to it and returned it to me an exemplary and timeless classic. You are a blessing. Thank you!

A special thanks to the executive teams of my organizations in LA and Denver for faithfully steering the ship during my writing retreats. You masterfully kept our many boats afloat, affording me the peace and focus needed to finish this important project. You all are very much a part of this success. God bless each of you.

Thank you to Amanda McIntire of the Mac Creative Agency for your continued excellent guidance in the cover and visuals for *Balance* and your strategic marketing input. You are peerless!

To Sarah, my wife and partner in everything I do. Babe, we did it again! Every win I have is not my own; it's ours. I'm better because your life is intertwined with mine. Thank you for your brilliance, your love, and being my chief sounding board. You're everything to me, baby. I love you.

To my children, Lauren, Teya, Isaiah, Malachi, Makenzie, and Ella. Thank you for being so understanding while I was either away writing or home but not as present as usual. Your selflessness contributed to this book tremendously. Thank *you*! I'm so proud of each of you, and you are the inspiration for every great thing I accomplish.

To my mother, Tommye Williams, who has held the title of my number one fan for more than four decades. Thank you for believing in me the way you do. You encourage the best parts of me. Your inspiration has been my guiding light for longer than I can remember. I love you. Thank you. Oh, and please give Aunt Yvette and Grandma Betty a big hug for me!

To my extended village, the Jakes family. Thank you for the love and support that is commonplace in our union. I'm better because we're connected. It's like we were—if you will allow me to use a double negative—never *not* family. I thank God for bringing us together.

Finally, I give the highest thanks to my creator and the shaper of my life. To my God, my best friend, my savior, my deliverer, my encourager, and the one who strengthens me. Jesus, you are my main ingredient. You have kept every promise you've made to me and beyond. I love you with all of my heart. I pray that *Balance* will draw every reader one step closer to you and the abundant, blessed, and balanced life you came to bring to humankind.

# Notes

1. Ps. 30:5.
2. Mark 8:36.
3. Tasha Eurich, "What Self-Awareness Really Is (and How to Cultivate It)," *Harvard Business Review* (January 4, 2018), https://hbr.org/2018/01/what -self-awareness-really-is-and-how-to-cultivate-it.
4. Ibid.
5. Neel Burton, "Our Hierarchy of Needs," *Psychology Today* (May 23, 2012), www.psychologytoday.com/us/blog/hide-and-seek/201205/our -hierarchy-needs.
6. Steven Kotler, "Three Science-Based Strategies to Increase Your Creativity," TED (January 28, 2021), https://ideas.ted.com/3-science -based-strategies-to-increase-your-creativity/.
7. Mark 8:37.
8. "Repetitive Negative Thinking Linked to Dementia Risk," UCL (June 8, 2020), www.ucl.ac.uk/news/2020/jun/repetitive-negative -thinking-linked-dementia-risk.
9. Touré Roberts, *Wholeness* (Grand Rapids: Zondervan, 2018).
10. Sarah Lewis, *The Rise: Creativity, the Gift of Failure, and the Search for Mastery* (New York: Simon and Schuster, 2015), 11–12.
11. "g0264. ἁμαρτάνω hamartano; perhaps from 1 (as a negative particle) and the base of 3313; properly, to miss the mark (and so not share in the prize), i.e. (figuratively) to err, especially (morally) to sin:—for your faults, offend, sin, trespass." *Strong's Exhaustive Concordance.*
12. "Millennials' Most Important Life Goal, by Financial Health," Marketing Charts, n.d., www.marketingcharts.com/industries/education-63794 /attachment/navient-millennials-most-important-life-goal-dec2015.

# Notes

13. Naomi Osaka, "It's O.K. Not to Be O.K.," *Time* (July 8, 2021), https://time.com/6077128/naomi-osaka-essay-tokyo-olympics/.
14. Exodus 14.
15. Toni Morrison, *Song of Solomon* (New York: Knopf, 1977).
16. Lewis, *The Rise*, 27–28.
17. Touré Roberts, *Purpose Awakening* (FaithWords, 2014).
18. Budd Davisson, "Pilots versus Aviators," *Plane and Pilot* (February 6, 2016), www.planeandpilotmag.com/article/pilots-versus-aviators/.
19. See www.toureroberts.com/thecalled.
20. Matt. 12:34.

# Wholeness

## Winning in Life from the Inside Out

*Touré Roberts*

*Wholeness* is about removing invisible boundaries from our lives that keep us from realizing our highest potential. In order to live an outer life without limits, we have to uncover and address the inner limitations that hide in our blind spots.

This life-changing book explains that regardless of where you are in life, Wholeness will take you higher. *Wholeness* will elevate your sense of fulfillment in life, produce healthier, more rewarding relationships, and will position you for optimum success in every endeavor.

International thought leader and pastor Touré Roberts explains we can't always choose the experiences that keep us from being whole, but we can take control of our lives today and bring healing to any broken area. Key chapters include an in-depth relationship guide titled "Two Halves Don't Make a Whole." "The Cracked Mirror" shows how unprocessed experiences can negatively shape our view of self, others, and the world around us. "Ghosts of the Past" gives powerful, practical tools for avoiding the traps of the past and ensuring that we enter into the amazing future that God has planned for us.

*Wholeness* is filled with wisdom garnered from Touré's own life—raised by a single mom, narrowly escaping the traps of inner-city life, and finding success in corporate America. His insight is further broadened by his role as founder of one of the most influential churches in the nation, with more than fourteen years pastoring thousands of millennials, couples, families, and a diverse group of individuals. *Wholeness* will take you on a transformational journey that won't leave you the same.

Concluding with a "Wholeness Test," *Wholeness* will help you track and maintain your progress while walking out your journey to your full potential.

*Available in stores and online!*